St. Louis Cardinals 2021

A Baseball Companion

Edited by Steven Goldman and Bret Sayre

Baseball Prospectus

Craig Brown, Associate Editor
Robert Au, Harry Pavlidis and Amy Pircher, Statistics Editors

Copyright © 2021 by DIY Baseball, LLC.
All rights reserved

This book or any part thereof may not be reproduced or transmitted in any form or by any means, electronic or mechanical, including photocopying, recording, or by any information storage and retrieval system, without permission in writing from the publisher.

Limit of Liability/Disclaimer of Warranty: While the publisher and the author have used their best efforts in preparing this book, they make no representations or warranties with respect to the accuracy or completeness of the contents of this book and specifically disclaim any implied warranties of merchantability or fitness for a particular purpose. No warranty may be created or extended by sales representatives or written sales materials. The advice and strategies contained herein may not be suitable for your situation. You should consult with a professional where appropriate. Neither the publisher nor the author shall be liable for any loss of profit or any other commercial damages, including but not limited to special, incidental, consequential, or other damages.

Library of Congress Cataloging-in-Publication Data:
paperback
ISBN-13: 978-1-950716-75-3

Project Credits
Cover Design: Ginny Searle
Interior Design and Production: Amy Pircher, Robert Au
Layout: Amy Pircher, Robert Au

Baseball icon courtesy of Uberux, from https://www.shareicon.net/author/uberux

Ballpark diagram courtesy of Lou Spirito/THIRTY81 Project, https://thirty81project.com/

Manufactured in the United States of America
10 9 8 7 6 5 4 3 2 1

Table of Contents

Statistical Introduction v

Part 1: Team Analysis

Performance Graphs 3
2020 Team Performance 4
2021 Team Projections 5
Team Personnel 6
Busch Stadium Stats 7
Cardinals Team Analysis 9

Part 2: Player Analysis

Cardinals Player Analysis 16
Cardinals Prospects 83

Part 3: Featured Articles

Cardinals All-Time Top 10 Players 95
   by Matthew Trueblood

A Taxonomy of 2020 Abnormalities 101
   by Rob Mains

Tranches of WAR 107
   by Russell A. Carleton

Secondhand Sport 113
   by Patrick Dubuque

Steve Dalkowski Dreaming 117
   by Steven Goldman

A Reward For A Functioning Society 121
   by Cory Frontin and Craig Goldstein

Index of Names 125

Statistical Introduction

Sports are, fundamentally, a blend of athletic endeavor and storytelling. Baseball, like any other sport, tells its stories in so many ways: in the arc of a game from the stands or a season from the box scores, in photos, or even in numbers. At Baseball Prospectus, we understand that statistics don't replace observation or any of baseball's stories, but complement everything else that makes the game so much fun.

What stats help us with is with patterns and precision, variance and value. This book can help you learn things you may not see from watching a game or hundred, whether it's the path of a career over time or the breadth of the entire MLB. We'd also never ask you to choose between our numbers and the experience of viewing a game from the cheap seats or the comfort of your home; our publication combines running the numbers with observations and wisdom from some of the brightest minds we can find. But if you *do* want to learn more about the numbers beyond what's on the backs of player jerseys, let us help explain.

Offense

We've revised our methodology for determining batting value. Long-time readers of the book will notice that we've retired True Average in favor of a new metric: Deserved Runs Created Plus (DRC+). Developed by Jonathan Judge and our stats team, this statistic measures everything a player does at the plate–reaching base, hitting for power, making outs, and moving runners over–and puts it on a scale where 100 equals league-average performance. A DRC+ of 150 is terrific, a DRC+ of 100 is average and a DRC+ of 75 means you better be an excellent defender.

DRC+ also does a better job than any of our previous metrics in taking contextual factors into account. The model adjusts for how the park affects performance, but also for things like the talent of the opposing pitcher, value of different types of batted-ball events, league, temperature and other factors. It's able to describe a player's expected offensive contribution than any other statistic we've found over the years, and also does a better job of predicting future performance as well.

The other aspect of run-scoring is baserunning, which we quantify using Baserunning Runs. BRR not only records the value of stolen bases (or getting caught in the act), but also accounts for all the stuff that doesn't show up on the back of a baseball card: a runner's ability to go first to third on a single, or advance on a fly ball.

Defense

Where offensive value is *relatively* easy to identify and understand, defensive value is … not. Over the past dozen years, the sabermetric community has focused mostly on stats based on zone data: a real-live human person records the type of batted ball and estimated landing location, and models are created that give expected outs. From there, you can compare fielders' actual outs to those expected ones. Simple, right?

Unfortunately, zone data has two major issues. First, zone data is recorded by commercial data providers who keep the raw data private unless you pay for it. (All the statistics we build in this book and on our website use public data as inputs.) That hurts our ability to test assumptions or duplicate results. Second, over the years it has become apparent that there's quite a bit of "noise" in zone-based fielding analysis. Sometimes the conclusions drawn from zone data don't hold up to scrutiny, and sometimes the different data provided by different providers don't look anything alike, giving wildly different results. Sometimes the hard-working professional stringers or scorers might unknowingly inflict unconscious bias into the mix: for example good fielders will often be credited with more expected outs despite the data, and ballparks with high press boxes tend to score more line drives than ones with a lower press box.

Enter our Fielding Runs Above Average (FRAA). For most positions, FRAA is built from play-by-play data, which allows us to avoid the subjectivity found in many other fielding metrics. The idea is this: count how many fielding plays are made by a given player and compare that to expected plays for an average fielder at their position (based on pitcher ground ball tendencies and batter handedness). Then we adjust for park and base-out situations.

When it comes to catchers, our methodology is a little different thanks to the laundry list of responsibilities they're tasked with beyond just, well, catching and throwing the ball. By now you've probably heard about "framing" or the art of making umpires more likely to call balls outside the strike zone for strikes. To put this into one tidy number, we incorporate pitch tracking data (for the years it exists) and adjust for important factors like pitcher, umpire, batter and home-field advantage using a mixed-model approach. This grants us a number for how many strikes the catcher is personally adding to (or subtracting from) his pitchers' performance … which we then convert to runs added or lost using linear weights.

Framing is one of the biggest parts of determining catcher value, but we also take into account blocking balls from going past, whether a scorer deems it a passed ball or a wild pitch. We use a similar approach—one that really benefits from the pitch tracking data that tells us what ends up in the dirt and what doesn't. We also include a catcher's ability to prevent stolen bases and how well they field balls in play, and *finally* we come up with our FRAA for catchers.

Pitching

Both pitching and fielding make up the half of baseball that isn't run scoring: run prevention. Separating pitching from fielding is a tough task, and most recent pitching analysis has branched off from Voros McCracken's famous (and controversial) statement, "There is little if any difference among major-league pitchers in their ability to prevent hits on balls hit in the field of play." The research of the analytic community has validated this to some extent, and there are a host of "defense-independent" pitching measures that have been developed to try and extract the effect of the defense behind a hurler from the pitcher's work.

Our solution to this quandary is Deserved Run Average (DRA), our core pitching metric. DRA seeks to evaluate a pitcher's performance, much like earned run average (ERA), the tried-and-true pitching stat you've seen on every baseball broadcast or box score from the past century, but it's very different. To start, DRA takes an event-by-event look at what the pitchers does, and adjusts the value of that event based on different environmental factors like park, batter, catcher, umpire, base-out situation, run differential, inning, defense, home field advantage, pitcher role and temperature. That mixed model gives us a pitcher's expected contribution, similar to what we do for our DRC+ model for hitters and FRAA model for catchers. (Oh, and we also consider the pitcher's effect on basestealing and on balls getting past the catcher.)

DRA is set to the scale of runs allowed per nine innings (RA9) instead of ERA, which makes DRA's scale slightly higher than ERA's. Because of this, for ease of use, we're supplying DRA-, which is much easier for the reader to parse. As with DRC+, DRA- is an "index" stat, meaning instead of using some arbitrary and shifting number to denote what's "good," average is always 100. The reason that it uses a minus rather than a plus is because like ERA, a lower number is better. Therefore a 75 DRA- describes a performance 25 percent better than average, whereas a 150 DRA- means that either a pitcher is getting extremely lucky with their results, or getting ready to try a new pitch.

Since the last time you picked up an edition of this book, we've also made a few minor changes to DRA to make it better. Recent research into "tunneling"—the act of throwing consecutive pitches that appear similar from a batter's point of view until after the swing decision point–data has given us a new contextual factor to account for in DRA: plate distance. This refers to the distance between successive pitches as they approach the plate, and while it has a smaller effect than factors like velocity or whiff rate, it still can help explain pitcher strikeout rate in our model.

Recently Added Descriptive Statistics

Returning to our 2021 edition of the book are a few figures which recently appeared. These numbers may be a little bit more familiar to those of you who have spent some time investigating baseball statistics.

Fastball Percentage

Our fastball percentage (FA%) statistic measures how frequently a pitcher throws a pitch classified as a "fastball," measured as a percentage of overall pitches thrown. We qualify three types of fastballs:

1. The traditional four-seam fastball;
2. The two-seam fastball or sinker;
3. "Hard cutters," which are pitches that have the movement profile of a cut fastball and are used as the pitcher's primary offering or in place of a more traditional fastball.

For example, a pitcher with a FA% of 67 throws any combination of these three pitches about two-thirds of the time.

Whiff Rate

Everybody loves a swing and a miss, and whiff rate (Whiff%) measures how frequently pitchers induce a swinging strike. To calculate Whiff%, we add up all the pitches thrown that ended with a swinging strike, then divide that number by a pitcher's total pitches thrown. Most often, high whiff rates correlate with high strikeout rates (and overall effective pitcher performance).

Called Strike Probability

Called Strike Probability (CSP) is a number that represents the likelihood that all of a pitcher's pitches will be called a strike while controlling for location, pitcher and batter handedness, umpire and count. Here's how it works: on each pitch, our model determines how many times (out of 100) that a similar pitch was called for a strike given those factors mentioned above, and when normalized for each batter's strike zone. Then we average the CSP for all pitches thrown by a pitcher in a season, and that gives us the yearly CSP percentage you see in the stats boxes.

As you might imagine, pitchers with a higher CSP are more likely to work in the zone, where pitchers with a lower CSP are likely locating their pitches outside the normal strike zone, for better or for worse.

Projections

Many of you aren't turning to this book just for a look at what a player has done, but for a look at what a player is going to do: the PECOTA projections. PECOTA, initially developed by Nate Silver (who has moved on to greater fame as a political analyst), consists of three parts:

1. Major-league equivalencies, which use minor-league statistics to project how a player will perform in the major leagues;
2. Baseline forecasts, which use weighted averages and regression to the mean to estimate a player's current true talent level; and
3. Aging curves, which uses the career paths of comparable players to estimate how a player's statistics are likely to change over time.

With all those important things covered, let's take a look at what's in the book this year.

Team Prospectus

Most of this book is composed of team chapters, with one for each of the 30 major-league franchises. On the first page of each chapter, you'll see a box that contains some of the key statistics for each team as well as a very inviting stadium diagram.

We start with the team name, their unadjusted 2020 win-loss record, and their divisional ranking. Beneath that are a host of other team statistics. **Pythag** presents an adjusted 2020 winning percentage, calculated by taking runs scored per game (**RS/G**) and runs allowed per game (**RA/G**) for the team, and running them through a version of Bill James' Pythagorean formula that was refined and improved by David Smyth and Brandon Heipp. (The formula is called "Pythagenpat," which is equally fun to type and to say.)

Next up is **DRC+**, described earlier, to indicate the overall hitting ability of the team either above or below league-average. Run prevention on the pitching side is covered by **DRA** (also mentioned earlier) and another metric: Fielding Independent Pitching (**FIP**), which calculates another ERA-like statistic based on strikeouts, walks, and home runs recorded. Defensive Efficiency Rating (**DER**) tells us the percentage of balls in play turned into outs for the team, and is a quick fielding shorthand that rounds out run prevention.

After that, we have several measures related to roster composition, as opposed to on-field performance. **B-Age** and **P-Age** tell us the average age of a team's batters and pitchers, respectively. **Payroll** is the combined team payroll for all on-field players, and Doug Pappas' Marginal Dollars per Marginal Win (**M$/MW**) tells us how much money a team spent to earn production above replacement level.

Next to each of these stats, we've listed each team's MLB rank in that category from first to 30th. In this, first always indicates a positive outcome and 30th a negative outcome, except in the case of salary—first is highest.

After the franchise statistics, we share a few items about the team's home ballpark. There's the aforementioned diagram of the park's dimensions (including distances to the outfield wall), a graphic showing the height of the wall from the left-field pole to the right-field pole, and a table showing three-year park factors for the stadium. The park factors are displayed as indexes where 100 is average, 110 means that the park inflates the statistic in question by 10 percent, and 90 means that the park deflates the statistic in question by 10 percent.

On the second page of each team chapter, you'll find three graphs. The first is **Payroll History** and helps you see how the team's payroll has compared to the MLB and divisional average payrolls over time. Payroll figures are current as of January 1, 2021; with so many free agents still unsigned as of this writing, the final 2021 figure will likely be significantly different for many teams. (In the meantime, you can always find the most current data at Baseball Prospectus' Cot's Baseball Contracts page.)

The second graph is **Future Commitments** and helps you see the team's future outlays, if any.

The third graph is **Farm System Ranking** and displays how the Baseball Prospectus prospect team has ranked the organization's farm system since 2007.

After the graphs, we have a **Personnel** section that lists many of the important decision-makers and upper-level field and operations staff members for the franchise, as well as any former Baseball Prospectus staff members who are currently part of the organization. (In very rare circumstances, someone might be on both lists!)

Position Players

After all that information and a thoughtful bylined essay covering each team, we present our player comments. These are also bylined, but due to frequent franchise shifts during the offseason, our bylines are more a rough guide than a perfect accounting of who wrote what.

Each player is listed with the major-league team that employed him as of early January 2021. If a player changed teams after that point via free agency, trade, or any other method, you'll be able to find them in the chapter for their previous squad.

As an example, take a look at the player comment for Padres shortstop Fernando Tatis Jr.: the stat block that accompanies his written comment is at the top of this page. First we cover biographical information (age is as of June 30, 2021) before moving onto the stats themselves. Our statistic columns include standard identifying information like **YEAR**, **TEAM**, **LVL** (level of affiliated play) and **AGE** before getting into the numbers. Next, we provide raw, untranslated

Fernando Tatis Jr. SS
Born: 01/02/99   Age: 22   Bats: R   Throws: R
Height: 6'3"   Weight: 217   Origin: International Free Agent, 2015

YEAR	TEAM	LVL	AGE	PA	R	2B	3B	HR	RBI	BB	K	SB	CS	AVG/OBP/SLG
2018	SA	AA	19	394	77	22	4	16	43	33	109	16	5	.286/.355/.507
2019	SD	MLB	20	372	61	13	6	22	53	30	110	16	6	.317/.379/.590
2020	SD	MLB	21	257	50	11	2	17	45	27	61	11	3	.277/.366/.571
2021 FS	SD	MLB	22	600	95	24	4	31	81	50	165	17	8	.263/.331/.499
2021 DC	SD	MLB	22	628	100	25	4	32	85	53	173	19	8	.263/.331/.499

Comparables: Darryl Strawberry, Bo Bichette, Ronald Acuña Jr.

YEAR	TEAM	LVL	AGE	PA	DRC+	BABIP	BRR	FRAA	WARP
2018	SA	AA	19	394	136	.370	3.0	SS(83): -1.9	2.4
2019	SD	MLB	20	372	118	.410	7.1	SS(83): 0.9	3.4
2020	SD	MLB	21	257	126	.306	0.7	SS(57): -5.5	0.9
2021 FS	SD	MLB	22	600	126	.318	1.7	SS -1	3.9
2021 DC	SD	MLB	22	628	126	.318	1.8	SS -1	4.0

numbers like you might find on the back of your dad's baseball cards: **PA** (plate appearances), **R** (runs), **2B** (doubles), **3B** (triples), **HR** (home runs), **RBI** (runs batted in), **BB** (walks), **K** (strikeouts), **SB** (stolen bases) and **CS** (caught stealing).

Following the basic stats is **Whiff%** (whiff rate), which denotes how often, when a batter swings, he fails to make contact with the ball. Another way to think of this number is an inverse of a hitter's contact rate.

Next, we have unadjusted "slash" statistics: **AVG** (batting average), **OBP** (on-base percentage) and **SLG** (slugging percentage). Following the slash line is **DRC+** (Deserved Runs Created Plus), which we described earlier as total offensive expected contribution compared to the league average.

BABIP (batting average on balls in play) tells us how often a ball in play fell for a hit, and can help us identify whether a batter may have been lucky or not … but note that high BABIPs also tend to follow the great hitters of our time, as well as speedy singles hitters who put the ball on the ground.

The next item is **BRR** (Baserunning Runs), which covers all of a player's baserunning accomplishments including (but not limited to) swiped bags and failed attempts. Next is **FRAA** (Fielding Runs Above Average), which also includes the number of games previously played at each position noted in parentheses. Multi-position players have only their two most frequent positions listed here, but their total FRAA number reflects all positions played.

Our last column here is **WARP** (Wins Above Replacement Player). WARP estimates the total value of a player, which means for hitters it takes into account hitting runs above average (calculated using the DRC+ model), BRR and FRAA. Then, it makes an adjustment for positions played and gives the player a credit for plate appearances based upon the difference between "replacement level"—which is derived from the quality of players added to a team's roster after the start of the season–and the league average.

The final line just below the stats box is **PECOTA** data, which is discussed further in a following section.

Catchers

Catchers are a special breed, and thus they have earned their own separate box which displays some of the defensive metrics that we've built just for them. As an example, let's check out Yasmani Grandal.

YEAR	TEAM	P. COUNT	FRM RUNS	BLK RUNS	THRW RUNS	TOT RUNS
2018	LAD	16816	15.7	0.8	0.1	16.5
2019	MIL	18740	19.4	1.8	-0.1	21.1
2020	CHW	4830	3.7	0.3	-0.2	3.8
2021	CHW	14430	16.7	-0.6	1.0	17.1
2021	CHW	14430	16.7	0.4	1.0	18.0

The **YEAR** and **TEAM** columns match what you'd find in the other stat box. **P. COUNT** indicates the number of pitches thrown while the catcher was behind the plate, including swinging strikes, fouls and balls in play. **FRM RUNS** is the total run value the catcher provided (or cost) his team by influencing the umpire to call strikes where other catchers did not. **BLK RUNS** expresses the total run value above or below average for the catcher's ability to prevent wild pitches and passed balls. **THRW RUNS** is calculated using a similar model as the previous two statistics, and it measures a catcher's ability to throw out basestealers but also to dissuade them from testing his arm in the first place. It takes into account factors like the pitcher (including his delivery and pickoff move) and baserunner (who could be as fast as Billy Hamilton or as slow as Yonder Alonso). **TOT RUNS** is the sum of all of the previous three statistics.

Pitchers

Let's give our pitchers a turn, using 2020 AL Cy Young winner Shane Bieber as our example. Take a look at his stat block: the first line and the **YEAR**, **TEAM**, **LVL** and **AGE** columns are the same as in the position player example earlier.

Here too, we have a series of columns that display raw, unadjusted statistics compiled by the pitcher over the course of a season: **W** (wins), **L** (losses), **SV** (saves), **G** (games pitched), **GS** (games started), **IP** (innings pitched), **H** (hits allowed) and **HR** (home runs allowed). Next we have two statistics that are rates: **BB/9** (walks per nine innings) and **K/9** (strikeouts per nine innings), before returning to the unadjusted K (strikeouts).

Next up is **GB%** (ground ball percentage), which is the percentage of all batted balls that were hit on the ground, including both outs and hits. Remember, this is based on observational data and subject to human error, so please approach this with a healthy dose of skepticism.

BABIP (batting average on balls in play) is calculated using the same methodology as it is for position players, but it often tells us more about a pitcher than it does a hitter. With pitchers, a high BABIP is often due to poor defense or bad luck, and can often be an indicator of potential rebound, and a low BABIP may be cause to expect performance regression. (A typical league-average BABIP is close to .290-.300.)

The metrics **WHIP** (walks plus hits per inning pitched) and **ERA** (earned run average) are old standbys: WHIP measures walks and hits allowed on a per-inning basis, while ERA measures earned runs on a nine-inning basis. Neither of these stats are translated or adjusted.

DRA- (Deserved Run Average) was described at length earlier, and measures how the pitcher "deserved" to perform compared to other pitchers. Please note that since we lack all the data points that would make for a "real" DRA for minor-league events, the DRA- displayed for minor league partial-seasons is based off of different data. (That data is a modified version of our cFIP metric, which you can find more information about on our website.)

Shane Bieber   RHP

Born: 05/31/95   Age: 26   Bats: R   Throws: R
Height: 6'3"   Weight: 200   Origin: Round 4, 2016 Draft (#122 overall)

YEAR	TEAM	LVL	AGE	W	L	SV	G	GS	IP	H	HR	BB/9	K/9	K	GB%	BABIP
2018	AKR	AA	23	3	0	0	5	5	31	26	1	0.3	8.7	30	47.3%	.278
2018	COL	AAA	23	3	1	0	8	8	48^2	30	3	1.1	8.7	47	52.0%	.227
2018	CLE	MLB	23	11	5	0	20	19	114^2	130	13	1.8	9.3	118	46.2%	.356
2019	CLE	MLB	24	15	8	0	34	33	214^1	186	31	1.7	10.9	259	44.4%	.298
2020	CLE	MLB	25	8	1	0	12	12	77^1	46	7	2.4	14.2	122	48.4%	.267
2021 FS	CLE	MLB	26	10	6	0	26	26	150	121	18	2.1	11.7	195	45.5%	.297
2021 DC	CLE	MLB	26	14	7	0	30	30	196.7	159	24	2.1	11.7	257	45.5%	.297

Comparables: Luis Severino, Danny Salazar, Joe Musgrove

YEAR	TEAM	LVL	AGE	WHIP	ERA	DRA-	WARP	MPH	FB%	WHF	CSP
2018	AKR	AA	23	0.87	1.16	61	0.9				
2018	COL	AAA	23	0.74	1.66	69	1.2				
2018	CLE	MLB	23	1.33	4.55	74	2.6	94.7	57.4%	26.2%	
2019	CLE	MLB	24	1.05	3.28	75	4.9	94.4	45.8%	30.8%	
2020	CLE	MLB	25	0.87	1.63	53	2.6	95.3	53.6%	40.7%	
2021 FS	CLE	MLB	26	1.04	2.44	64	4.4	94.7	50.0%	33.2%	44.2%
2021 DC	CLE	MLB	26	1.04	2.44	64	5.8	94.7	50.0%	33.2%	44.2%

Just like with hitters, **WARP** (Wins Above Replacement Player) is a total value metric that puts pitchers of all stripes on the same scale as position players. We use DRA as the primary input for our calculation of WARP. You might notice that relief pitchers (due to their limited innings) may have a lower WARP than you were expecting or than you might see in other WARP-like metrics. WARP does not take leverage into account, just the actions a pitcher performs and the expected value of those actions ... which ends up judging high-leverage relief pitchers differently than you might imagine given their prestige and market value.

MPH gives you the pitcher's 95th percentile velocity for the noted season, in order to give you an idea of what the *peak* fastball velocity a pitcher possesses. Since this comes from our pitch-tracking data, it is not publicly available for minor-league pitchers.

Finally, we display the three new pitching metrics we described earlier. **FB%** (fastball percentage) gives you the percentage of fastballs thrown out of all pitches. **WHF** (whiff rate) tells you the percentage of swinging strikes induced out of all pitches. **CSP** (called strike probability) expresses the likelihood of all pitches thrown to result in a called strike, after controlling for factors like handedness, umpire, pitch type, count and location.

PECOTA

All players have PECOTA projections for 2021, as well as a set of other numbers that describe the performance of comparable players according to PECOTA. All projections for 2021 are for the player at the date we went to press in early January and are projected into the league and park context as indicated by the team abbreviation. (Note that players at very low levels of the minors are too unpredictable to assess using these numbers.) All PECOTA projected statistics represent a player's projected major-league performance.

How we're doing that is a little different this season. There are really two different values that go into the final stat line that you see for PECOTA: How a player performs, and how much playing time he'll be given to perform it. In the past we've estimated playing time based on each team's roster and depth charts, and we'll continue to do that. These projections are denoted as **2021 DC**.

But in many cases, a player won't be projected for major-league playing time; most of the time this is because they aren't projected to be major-league players at all, but still developing as prospects. Or perhaps a player will provide Triple-A depth, only to have an opportunity open up because of injury. For these purposes, we're also supplying a second projection, labeled **2021 FS**, or full season. This is what we would project the player to provide in 600 plate appearances or 150 innings pitched.

Below the projections are the player's three highest-scoring comparable players as determined by PECOTA. All comparables represent a snapshot of how the listed player was performing at the same age as the current player, so if a

23-year-old pitcher is compared to Bartolo Colón, he's actually being compared to a 23-year-old Colón, not the version that pitched for the Rangers in 2018, nor to Colón's career as a whole.

A few points about pitcher projections. First, we aren't yet projecting peak velocity, so that column will be blank in the PECOTA lines. Second, projecting DRA is trickier than evaluating past performance, because it is unclear how deserving each pitcher will be of his anticipated outcomes. However, we know that another DRA-related statistic–contextual FIP or cFIP-estimates future run scoring very well. So for PECOTA, the projected DRA- figures you see are based on the past cFIPs generated by the pitcher and comparable players over time, along with the other factors described above.

If you're familiar with PECOTA, then you'll have noticed that the projection system often appears bullish on players coming off a bad year and bearish on players coming off a good year. (This is because the system weights several previous seasons, not just the most recent one.) In addition, we publish the 50th percentile projections for each player–which is smack in the middle of the range of projected production—which tends to mean PECOTA stat lines don't often have extreme results like 40 home runs or 250 strikeouts in a given season. In essence, PECOTA doesn't project very many extreme seasons.

Managers

After all those wonderful team chapters, we've got statistics for each big-league manager, all of whom are organized by alphabetical order. Here you'll find a block including an extraordinary amount of information collected from each manager's entire career. For more information on the acronyms and what they mean, please visit the Glossary at www.baseballprospectus.com.

There is one important metric that we'd like to call attention to, and you'll find it next to each manager's name: **wRM+** (weighted reliever management plus). Developed by Rob Arthur and Rian Watt, wRM+ investigates how good a manager is at using their best relievers during the moments of highest leverage, using both our proprietary DRA metric as well as Leverage Index. wRM+ is scaled to a league average of 100, and a wRM+ of 105 indicates that relievers were used approximately five percent "better" than average. On the other hand, a wRM+ of 95 would tell us the team used its relievers five percent "worse" than the average team.

While wRM+ does not have an extremely strong correlation with a manager, it is statistically significant; this means that a manager is not *entirely* responsible for a team's wRM+, but does have some effect on that number.

Part 1: Team Analysis

Performance Graphs

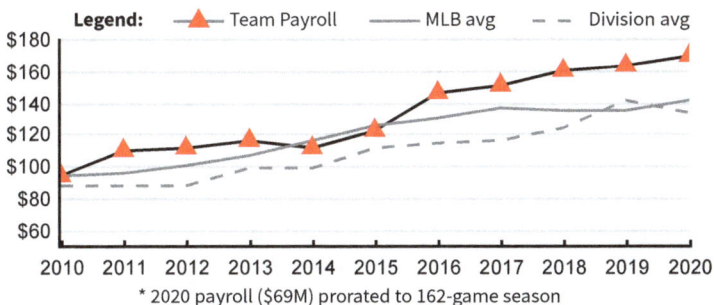

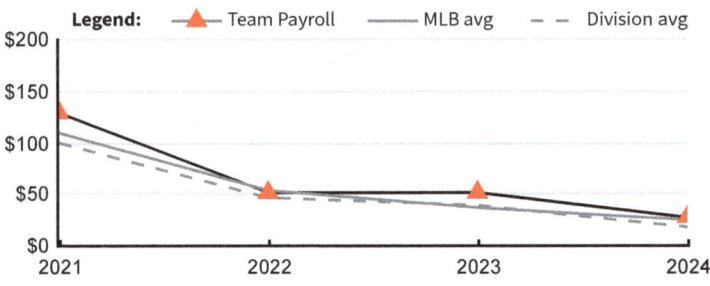

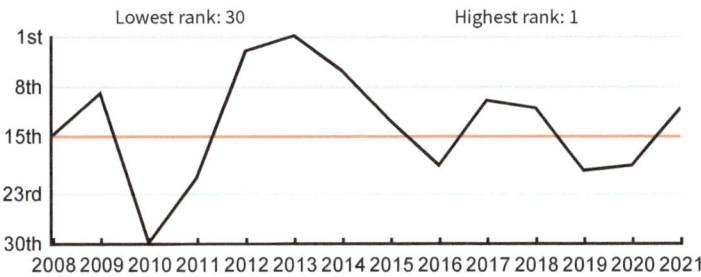

2020 Team Performance

ACTUAL STANDINGS

Team	W	L	Pct
CHC	34	26	0.567
CIN	31	29	0.517
STL	**30**	**28**	**0.517**
MIL	29	31	0.483
PIT	19	41	0.317

dWIN% STANDINGS

Team	W	L	Pct
CIN	32	28	0.537
MIL	29	31	0.496
CHC	27	33	0.465
STL	**26**	**34**	**0.436**
PIT	20	40	0.344

TOP HITTERS

Player	WARP
Kolten Wong	1.5
Paul Goldschmidt	1.3
Tyler O'Neill	0.9

TOP PITCHERS

Player	WARP
Adam Wainwright	0.7
Jack Flaherty	0.7
Dakota Hudson	0.6

VITAL STATISTICS

Statistic Name	Value	Rank
Pythagenpat	.521	11th
dWin%	.436	19th
Runs Scored per Game	4.14	24th
Runs Allowed per Game	3.95	6th
Deserved Runs Created Plus	94	23rd
Deserved Run Average Minus	95	12th
Fielding Independent Pitching	4.62	19th
Defensive Efficiency Rating	.735	1st
Batter Age	29.5	22nd
Pitcher Age	28.4	15th
Payroll	$69.0M	9th
Marginal $ per Marginal Win	$4.1M	18th

2021 Team Projections

PROJECTED STANDINGS

Team	W	L	Pct	+/-
MIL	89.1	72.9	0.550	10
Adding Kolten Wong doesn't quite make this an above-average lineup, but it improves their run prevention. Playoff hopes hinge on Christian Yelich being himself again.				
CHC	84.9	77.1	0.524	-6
Change, though painful, will give them an overdue chance to evaluate new options.				
STL	**80.4**	**81.6**	**0.496**	**0**
Nolan Arenado makes them favorites in the NL Central, but real parity with the goliaths on the coasts is still a ways off.				
CIN	79.3	82.7	0.490	-4
Traded or non-tendered several key role players to save money, and their Cy Young winner left as a free agent.				
PIT	59.5	102.5	0.367	8
This year will be about sorting out shortstop, hoping for progress from Mitch Keller, and enjoying Ke'Bryan Hayes--but not much more.				

TOP PROJECTED HITTERS

Player	WARP
Nolan Arenado	4.2
Paul Goldschmidt	3.6
Harrison Bader	2.0

TOP PROJECTED PITCHERS

Player	WARP
Jack Flaherty	3.7
Miles Mikolas	2.0
Kwang Hyun Kim	1.6

FARM SYSTEM REPORT

Top Prospect	Number of Top 101 Prospects
Dylan Carlson, #16	4

KEY DEDUCTIONS

Player	WARP
Kolten Wong	3.0
Austin Gomber	0.8
Dexter Fowler	0.6
John Brebbia	0.3

KEY ADDITIONS

Player	WARP
Nolan Arenado	4.2

Team Personnel

President of Baseball Operations
John Mozeliak

Vice President & General Manager
Mike Girsch

Assistant General Manager
Moises Rodriguez

Assistant General Manager & Director of Scouting
Randy Flores

Manager
Mike Shildt

BP Alumni
Zach Mortimer
Christopher Rodriguez
Mauricio Rubio

Busch Stadium Stats

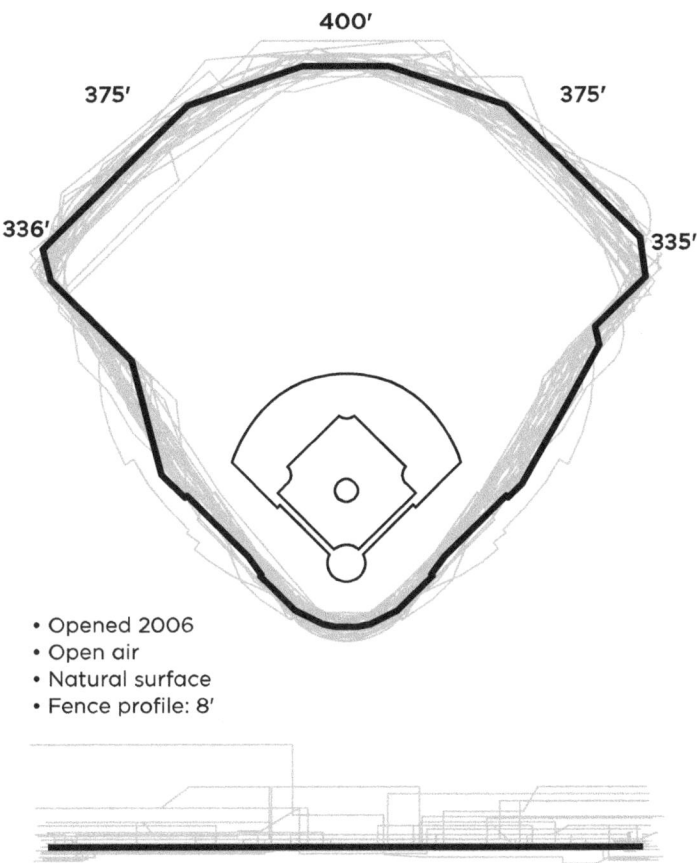

- Opened 2006
- Open air
- Natural surface
- Fence profile: 8'

Three-Year Park Factors

Runs	Runs/RH	Runs/LH	HR/RH	HR/LH
96	96	96	91	98

Cardinals Team Analysis

To quote one-half of the legendary rap group OutKast:

> "Baby boy, you only funky as your last cut
> You focus on the past, your ass'll be a 'has-what"

If that isn't a perfect verse to describe the St. Louis Cardinals, then I don't know what is.

St. Louis loves talking about the generations of tradition and success that have littered its organizational record books. There's even a book passed around to players in the franchise called "The Cardinal Way." It serves as one part instruction manual to detail what is expected of you based on the illustrious history of past players, and one part guide book to point players in the right direction with game-related questions.

For the past seven years, the Cardinals have ranked in the top three in attendance because of that tradition. Hell, that tradition is part of what sucked me into becoming a fan of the team in the first place. The first time I visited Busch Stadium it was like that moment when Harry Potter first lays his eyes on Hogwarts, in all its enormity and magic. Everything about the ballpark feels steeped in tradition and history. From the statues of all-time greats Stan Musial, Lou Brock and Bob Gibson on the corner of Clark Ave. and 8th Street, to the 11 World Series banners and 23 National League pennants displayed around the ballpark that signify that this isn't just any old ball club.

You can tell St. Louis is a city serious about baseball and its support of the Cardinals from the moment you immerse yourself in the atmosphere. But that history can only carry them so far, and while the Cardinals have benefited from it in the form of ticket sales, fan-generated revenue and championships in the past, it has also made them susceptible to making more mistakes of late when it comes to the product on the field.

It's easy to take your eye off the ball when you're among the most valuable baseball franchises in the league. But like OutKast said, the Cardinals are only as funky as their last cut, and the fact of the matter is, since winning 100 games in 2016, which resulted in a disappointing divisional round playoff loss, St. Louis has been an average ball club that is still resting on the achievements of past teams, rather than focusing on the future.

Take, for instance, when St. Louis tried to pitch itself to Giancarlo Stanton in 2017. The angle the front office reportedly used was focusing on tradition and the past championships the Cardinals have won. But Stanton wanted to hear about the future and what this team can do going forward. In the end, harping on what was wasn't enough to convince Stanton to waive his no-trade clause, and the two-time Silver Slugger ended up on a Yankees team with an incredibly bright future.

It's evidence that the history and strong branding the Cardinals have built going back decades isn't enough to sell the biggest-named players in the league on their team. The team responded by acquiring Paul Goldschmidt via trade, a move that, after a worrying first season, deserves praise. But the very fact that the Cardinals were forced to expend resources to obtain a star, rather than sign one through free agency, is telling. The product on the field needs to match the messaging of the franchise, and right now that's not happening.

In regard to the players the Cardinals have brought in recently, either through trade or free agency, there've been quite a few who haven't lived up to expectation. Marcell Ozuna is the most recent example. Ozuna was traded to the Cardinals when the Miami Marlins were holding their latest fire sale. After posting back-to-back All-Star seasons in Miami, complete with a Gold Glove and Silver Slugger award, St. Louis thought he would solve its lack of a big bat in the lineup. After all, Ozuna was just coming off a season in which he smacked 37 home runs.

Instead, in the two seasons he had in St. Louis, his production took a dip. He wasn't as dominant as he was in Miami, and it showed across almost every major statistical category at the plate. His slugging percentage dropped, his on-base percentage fell from .350 the prior two seasons with Miami, to .327 with St. Louis. His DRC+ fell accordingly, as his 109 and 111 figures, while still above average, paled in comparison to the 134 he had just recorded with the Marlins. His defense, whether truly deserving of a Gold Glove or not when with Miami, deteriorated significantly over his tenure in St. Louis.

What is interesting about Ozuna, though, is after the Cards decided not to bring him back as a free agent before the start of the 2020 season, he joined the Atlanta Braves, where he went on to have one of the best seasons of his career. He led the league in home runs and RBI, and had an eye-popping on-base percentage of .431 to go along with a .338 batting average, resulting in a 151 DRC+, good for fourth in the majors and tied with Mike Trout.

And that's not the first time a Cardinals player left the organization after suboptimal production, and found significant success with another team. Tommy Pham certainly comes to mind, as does Dexter Fowler. Watching the Fowler experience unfold is especially resonant of Ozuna. After five straight seasons of above-league average offensive production, Fowler had a strong initial season with St. Louis before watching his offense all but disappear. He's rebounded a bit the last two seasons, but not anywhere approaching his previous highs. It's fair to say he's underwhelmed both at the plate and in the field while battling through injuries that have repeatedly cost him time.

There's also Mike Leake, who the Cardinals paid big money to be an anchor in the rotation, though he never lived up to the contract. St. Louis signed the veteran pitcher to a five-year, $80 million deal, and after posting ERAs of 4.69 in 2016, and 4.29 in the first half of 2017, St. Louis traded him (and some of his salary) to the Mariners with little to show for it.

The Cardinals are far from the only team that has whiffed on signings and trades, but for a franchise that has historically seen more success than failure in that arena, the moves made in the last five years are especially jarring.

It's also not the only area where the Cardinals have struggled recently. St. Louis used to be a franchise that were kings of the process in developing players and finding the diamonds in the rough. It was evident enough that they inspired the hashtag #CardinalsDevilMagic, suggesting they were so good at turning nothing into something, there must be some dark arts involved. For years, the Cardinals farm system ranked among the best in the league despite their winning records, but recently, they've turned into a farm system for other teams, who continue to steal promising prospects in exchange for minimal success.

It's still early, but the name Randy Arozarena might haunt the Cardinals for years to come. The 25-year-old outfielder made a name for himself during the playoffs when he broke the record for most home runs by a rookie in a single postseason (seven), and followed that up by setting a new big-league record for most homers in one postseason (10). To top it off, he also set single-postseason records for hits (29) and total bases (64). By the time the World Series was over, it almost felt like Arozarena was the Rays' offense.

But before he became a household name with Tampa Bay, Arozarena was buried on the Cardinals bench or playing Triple-A ball, where he hit .396 in 2018 and .358 in 2019. Meanwhile, St. Louis was scratching its head trying to figure out how to make a dollar out of 15 cents with outfielders like Harrison Bader, who was hitting .200 at the time.

Context is key: The Cardinals traded Arozarena for coveted pitching prospect Matthew Liberatore (who could end up being phenomenal in a few years), but president of baseball operations John Mozeliak did admit fault in trading Arozarena after seeing him burst out in the postseason, saying "we will revisit how we rank our own players and make sure that we don't have something like this happen again."

That may be true, but it still doesn't take the sting away from that trade. Especially when you consider that he got just 23 plate appearances in 2019, while Bader (84 DRC+), José Martinez (94), and Yairo Muñoz (73)—all of whom came up through St. Louis' farm system as well—were underwhelming for long stretches of time on offense. That's a clear oversight by a franchise that typically prides itself on being the best at identifying talent.

St. Louis failed to give Arozarena a big enough opportunity in the majors to show what he could do, and instead hoped to get production out of guys who hadn't been consistent.

It's also not the first time the Cardinals have misevaluated their own talent, whether that's trading Tommy Pham, whose OPS would've been a ray of sunshine in St. Louis' lineup prior to 2020, underestimating Luke Voit's abilities, or sticking too long with Matt Carpenter at third base when Tommy Edman was clearly better defensively, running the bases and at the plate in most statistical categories.

The Pham situation, though, is the perfect example of the Cardinals not having a great handle on its own talent. Pham was traded essentially to make room for the excess in outfielding talent that existed within the Cardinals farm system, along with some rumblings of discord between the player and the front office. But it's been two years since that trade happened and St. Louis is still hurting for quality outfielders.

Munoz was cut after he ghosted the franchise over frustrations with how he was being used, Martinez was traded with Arozarena to the Rays for Liberatore, and while Bader and Tyler O'Neill may be great defenders, their performances at the dish raise doubts about their usefulness, especially in a lineup already devoid of a ton of hitting power.

How does a franchise that was once dominant at identifying great talent within its own farm system fail to see that their in-house replacements suddenly compound problems by bringing in talent that doesn't peak while trading away talent that does?? It's a problem that St. Louis needs to solve in a hurry.

It would be remiss not to mention the fact that the Cardinals did make a trip to the NLCS in 2019 against the eventual champion Washington Nationals. St. Louis also still managed to make the postseason last year after having to postpone a good portion of its schedule due to a COVID-19 outbreak within the locker room, and pushed the San Diego Padres to three games in the Wild Card round.

But the Cardinals have never been known to be a franchise satisfied with just making the postseason, or just making it out of the Wild Card round. This is not the Pittsburgh Pirates essay. Past success keeps fans coming out in droves to Busch Stadium, but it won't keep them there if the Cardinals continue to rest on their laurels of being a once dominant ball club. Otherwise, more players like Arozarena will slip through the cracks, and guys like Stanton will be unimpressed with their sales pitches because instead of being focused on the future, they'll still be talking about the past. Fortunately, flags fly forever, even the sepia-toned ones.

—*Jasmyn Wimbish is an author for CBS Sports.*

Part 2: Player Analysis

PLAYER COMMENTS WITH GRAPHS

Nolan Arenado 3B
Born: 04/16/91   Age: 30   Bats: R   Throws: R
Height: 6'2"   Weight: 215   Origin: Round 2, 2009 Draft (#59 overall)

YEAR	TEAM	LVL	AGE	PA	R	2B	3B	HR	RBI	BB	K	SB	CS	AVG/OBP/SLG
2018	COL	MLB	27	673	104	38	2	38	110	73	122	2	2	.297/.374/.561
2019	COL	MLB	28	662	102	31	2	41	118	62	93	3	2	.315/.379/.583
2020	COL	MLB	29	201	23	9	0	8	26	15	20	0	0	.253/.303/.434
2021 FS	STL	MLB	30	600	88	28	2	29	89	54	93	2	2	.277/.344/.507
2021 DC	STL	MLB	30	595	87	28	2	29	89	54	92	2	2	.277/.344/.507

Comparables: Ryan Zimmerman, Eric Chavez, Aramis Ramirez

This may have been the only case of a superstar whose swing opted out of the season without telling his body. After five straight years of the type of small-market MVP baseball that would make George Brett blush, Arenado had the power but not the groove. His DRC+ fell off a cliff—and in Denver it'll be impossible to narrow down which one it was—before a bum shoulder put an exclamation mark of dung onto his 2020. It's best not to read much into 200 plate appearances when the previous 3000 told a much different story, such as being the active leader among third basemen in slugging percentage. He still made his highlight plays. His batting discipline numbers all stayed the same. Maybe he was just put off by all the lifeless cardboard cutouts, like the rest of us.

YEAR	TEAM	LVL	AGE	PA	DRC+	BABIP	BRR	FRAA	WARP
2018	COL	MLB	27	673	137	.314	-2.9	3B(152): 9.1	6.2
2019	COL	MLB	28	662	135	.312	2.0	3B(154): 14.2	7.1
2020	COL	MLB	29	201	114	.241	0.4	3B(48): 5.3	1.5
2021 FS	STL	MLB	30	600	136	.283	-0.5	3B 3	4.2
2021 DC	STL	MLB	30	595	136	.283	-0.5	3B 3	4.2

Nolan Arenado, continued

Batted Ball Distribution

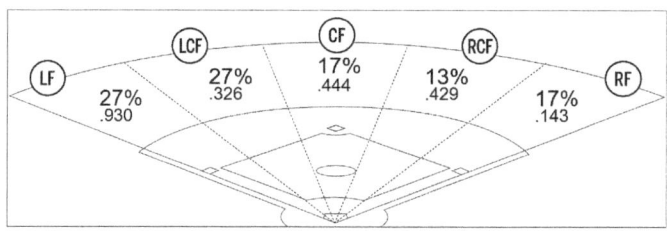

Strike Zone vs LHP   Strike Zone vs RHP

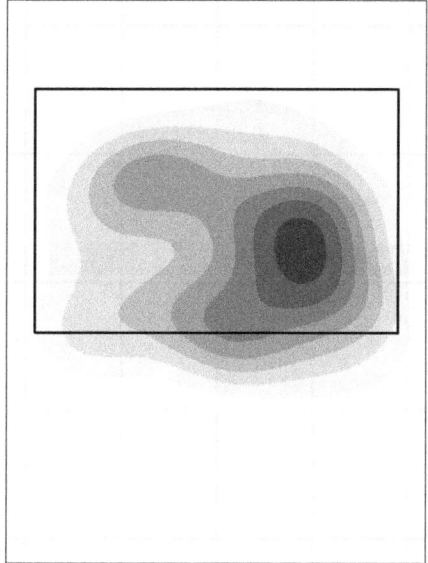

Harrison Bader CF

Born: 06/03/94   Age: 27   Bats: R   Throws: R
Height: 6'0"   Weight: 210   Origin: Round 3, 2015 Draft (#100 overall)

YEAR	TEAM	LVL	AGE	PA	R	2B	3B	HR	RBI	BB	K	SB	CS	AVG/OBP/SLG
2018	STL	MLB	24	427	61	20	2	12	37	31	125	15	3	.264/.334/.422
2019	MEM	AAA	25	75	23	3	0	7	15	8	16	3	0	.317/.427/.698
2019	STL	MLB	25	406	54	14	3	12	39	46	117	11	3	.205/.314/.366
2020	STL	MLB	26	125	21	7	2	4	11	13	40	3	1	.226/.336/.443
2021 FS	STL	MLB	27	600	73	22	2	21	68	50	187	9	5	.226/.311/.399
2021 DC	STL	MLB	27	458	56	16	2	16	52	38	143	7	4	.226/.311/.399

Comparables: Ruben Rivera, Larry Hisle, Drew Stubbs

Bader is a good boy, yes he is, who plays with the energy, enthusiasm and natural athleticism of a golden retriever. He bounds around the bases with reckless abandon and lives to chase down balls in the gap and finish innings with a dive, a catch, an impish grin and a contented trot back to the dugout. However, breaking stuff can leave him nosing through the azaleas in a confused and futile search for that tennis ball you only pretended to throw. Bader isn't a hacker so much as a guy who works deeps counts and gets fooled too often, leading to strikeouts in almost a third of his plate appearances last year. Everything else in his game is trending in the right direction, and Bader's combination of superlative defense, speed, walks and occasional power should make him a solid regular even if his two-strike approach never improves—and, as a result, he should be the recipient of plenty of boops on the nose, with the occasional belly rub mixed in.

YEAR	TEAM	LVL	AGE	PA	DRC+	BABIP	BRR	FRAA	WARP
2018	STL	MLB	24	427	90	.358	2.8	CF(74): 9.1, RF(38): 1.6, LF(6): 0.1	2.2
2019	MEM	AAA	25	75	157	.325	1.4	CF(16): 1.7	1.0
2019	STL	MLB	25	406	83	.268	4.5	CF(122): 14.4	2.5
2020	STL	MLB	26	125	85	.317	-0.7	CF(49): -3.6	-0.4
2021 FS	STL	MLB	27	600	100	.301	0.5	CF 7, LF 0	2.6
2021 DC	STL	MLB	27	458	100	.301	0.4	CF 5	2.0

Harrison Bader, continued

Batted Ball Distribution

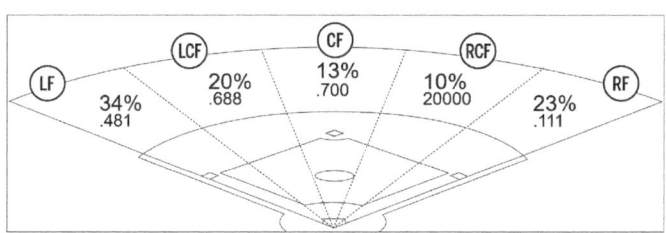

Strike Zone vs LHP   **Strike Zone vs RHP**

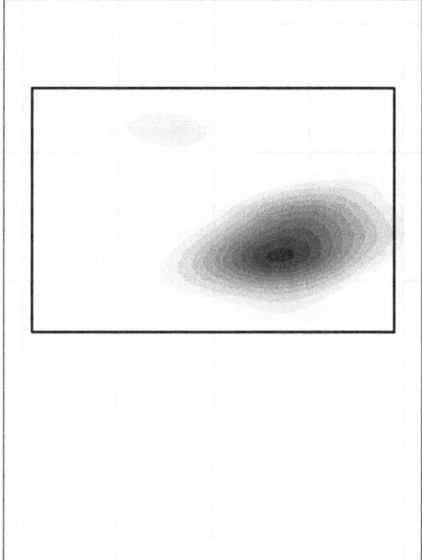

St. Louis Cardinals 2021

Dylan Carlson RF

Born: 10/23/98   Age: 22   Bats: S   Throws: L
Height: 6'2"   Weight: 205   Origin: Round 1, 2016 Draft (#33 overall)

YEAR	TEAM	LVL	AGE	PA	R	2B	3B	HR	RBI	BB	K	SB	CS	AVG/OBP/SLG
2018	PEO	LO-A	19	57	5	3	0	2	9	10	10	2	0	.234/.368/.426
2018	PMB	HI-A	19	441	63	19	3	9	53	52	78	6	3	.247/.345/.386
2019	SPR	AA	20	483	81	24	6	21	59	52	98	18	7	.281/.364/.518
2019	MEM	AAA	20	79	14	4	2	5	9	6	18	2	1	.361/.418/.681
2020	STL	MLB	21	119	11	7	1	3	16	8	35	1	1	.200/.252/.364
2021 FS	STL	MLB	22	600	69	22	3	19	68	50	180	4	2	.218/.288/.379
2021 DC	STL	MLB	22	546	63	20	3	17	62	45	164	3	2	.218/.288/.379

Comparables: Colby Rasmus, Nomar Mazara, Lastings Milledge

When St. Louis nabbed Carlson in the 2016 draft, he became the 10th outfielder or corner man they've chosen in the first round this century. None of the previous nine have posted a 2-win year in Redbird laundry, and only a handful of Piscotty and Rasmus joints earned even a single win, which proves that Cardinals Devil Magic can't always overcome the perpetual drag of drafting late. As for Carlson, look past the ugly numbers he put up as a 21-year-old rookie, trust your eyes and bet on him breaking the pattern. After an early September demotion to clear his head, the young switch-hitter showcased the approach, power and bat-to-ball skills of a future middle-of-the-order force. Carlson has good wheels and can handle center field but is a plus defender in a corner, where he'll be a value-priced building block for the next half-decade.

YEAR	TEAM	LVL	AGE	PA	DRC+	BABIP	BRR	FRAA	WARP
2018	PEO	LO-A	19	57	134	.257	-0.7	RF(10): 2.3, CF(4): -0.3	0.4
2018	PMB	HI-A	19	441	113	.286	1.7	RF(50): 4.7, LF(37): -0.1, CF(1): -0.1	1.2
2019	SPR	AA	20	483	150	.315	3.1	CF(87): -10.2, RF(9): -0.3, LF(5): -0.5	2.7
2019	MEM	AAA	20	79	141	.429	0.1	CF(8): -0.5, LF(7): 0.0, RF(3): -0.2	0.6
2020	STL	MLB	21	119	80	.260	-0.4	RF(18): 1.8, CF(17): -0.8, LF(10): -0.3	0.2
2021 FS	STL	MLB	22	600	86	.285	-0.1	RF 5, CF 0	1.0
2021 DC	STL	MLB	22	546	86	.285	0.0	RF 5, CF 0	0.7

Dylan Carlson, continued

Batted Ball Distribution

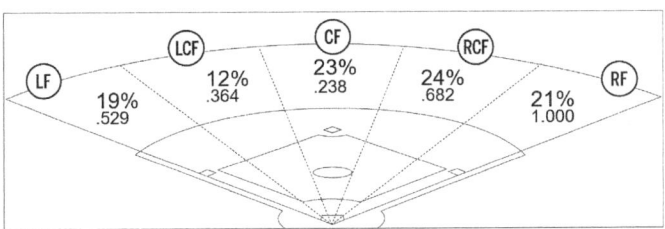

Strike Zone vs LHP   Strike Zone vs RHP

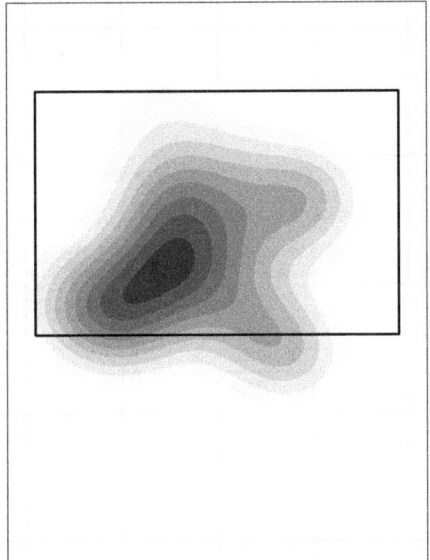

Matt Carpenter 3B

Born: 11/26/85 Age: 35 Bats: L Throws: R
Height: 6'4" Weight: 210 Origin: Round 13, 2009 Draft (#399 overall)

YEAR	TEAM	LVL	AGE	PA	R	2B	3B	HR	RBI	BB	K	SB	CS	AVG/OBP/SLG
2018	STL	MLB	32	677	111	42	0	36	81	102	158	4	1	.257/.374/.523
2019	STL	MLB	33	492	59	20	2	15	46	63	129	6	1	.226/.334/.392
2020	STL	MLB	34	169	22	6	0	4	24	23	48	0	0	.186/.325/.314
2021 FS	STL	MLB	35	600	76	25	1	19	65	85	167	3	2	.211/.335/.386
2021 DC	STL	MLB	35	550	70	23	1	18	59	78	153	3	2	.211/.335/.386

Comparables: Howard Johnson, Scott Rolen, Eric Chavez

"I'm a dog chasing cars. I wouldn't know what to do with one if I caught it!" Heath Ledger's Joker (still the best) said that, but it could just as well have been the current incarnation of Carpenter. The former 13th-round pick has built an impressive career out of grinding through at-bats, waiting for a pitch he can handle and putting a hurt on it. Carpenter's plate discipline and batting eye remain top shelf, and he still earns his free passes and sorts through buckets of pitches looking for the one with his name on it. But these days Carpenter doesn't know what to do with the meatballs he does catch, bouncing them harmlessly into the shift or swinging through them en route to a career-worst strikeout rate. His glove has become a millstone, and while the designated hitter came to the Senior Circuit last year the limited demand for a designated walker is unlikely to extend Carpenter's career as an everyday player. His peak was a joy to behold, but as he enters the back half of his 30s he's best cast as a professional pinch-hitter and veteran clubhouse presence.

YEAR	TEAM	LVL	AGE	PA	DRC+	BABIP	BRR	FRAA	WARP
2018	STL	MLB	32	677	135	.291	-1.5	1B(95): -3.6, 3B(76): 4.8, 2B(11): -0.6	4.6
2019	STL	MLB	33	492	95	.285	-1.9	3B(107): -6.5, 1B(4): -0.2	0.7
2020	STL	MLB	34	169	98	.250	0.0	3B(30): 4.2, 1B(6): -0.3	0.6
2021 FS	STL	MLB	35	600	102	.272	-0.5	3B 0, 2B -1	1.1
2021 DC	STL	MLB	35	550	102	.272	-0.5	3B 0, 2B -1	1.0

Matt Carpenter, continued

Batted Ball Distribution

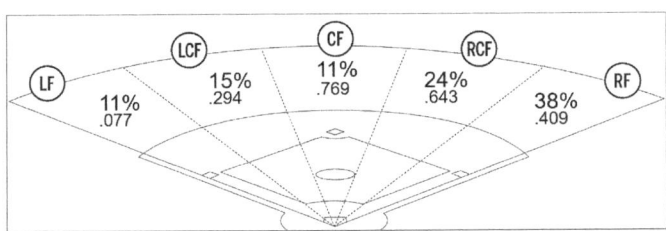

Strike Zone vs LHP   Strike Zone vs RHP

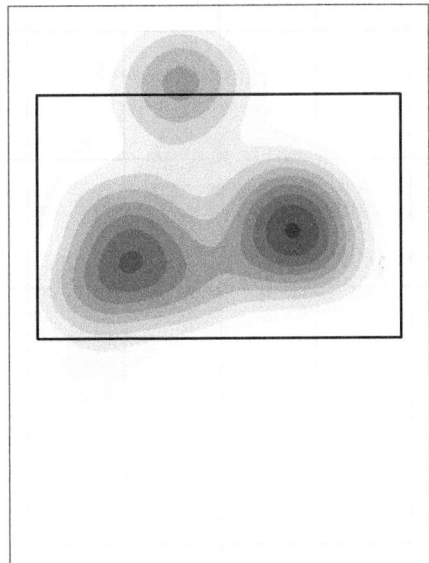

Paul DeJong SS

Born: 08/02/93   Age: 27   Bats: R   Throws: R
Height: 6'0"   Weight: 205   Origin: Round 4, 2015 Draft (#131 overall)

YEAR	TEAM	LVL	AGE	PA	R	2B	3B	HR	RBI	BB	K	SB	CS	AVG/OBP/SLG
2018	STL	MLB	24	490	68	25	1	19	68	36	123	1	1	.241/.313/.433
2019	STL	MLB	25	664	97	31	1	30	78	62	149	9	5	.233/.318/.444
2020	STL	MLB	26	174	17	6	0	3	25	17	50	1	0	.250/.322/.349
2021 FS	STL	MLB	27	600	74	22	1	24	77	47	171	2	2	.229/.300/.416
2021 DC	STL	MLB	27	594	73	22	1	24	76	47	169	2	2	.229/.300/.416

Comparables: Jhonny Peralta, Corey Seager, Bobby Crosby

A plus defensive shortstop with serious juice in his bat, DeJong has already blasted more home runs than all other Normal residents combined, which makes the Illinois State alum's power outage last year a bit of a mystery. His swings were even whiffier than usual, but when he did make contact DeJong lofted as many flyballs and smacked them just as hard as he has in the past. So, why did almost all of them settle into outfielders' gloves? Because he got a little underneath most of them, causing his rate of home runs per flyball to crater. Unless you're a Giancarlo-class Natural Born Slugger, that's a metric prone to great variation over time. With a few small adjustments and a little luck DeJong should be back launching bombs with aplomb next year; like most of us, then, he'd be wise to toss 2020 in the memory hole and work toward a more normal future.

YEAR	TEAM	LVL	AGE	PA	DRC+	BABIP	BRR	FRAA	WARP
2018	STL	MLB	24	490	101	.288	3.1	SS(114): 0.3	2.7
2019	STL	MLB	25	664	103	.259	0.5	SS(157): 7.1	4.2
2020	STL	MLB	26	174	87	.340	0.4	SS(45): -3.2	-0.1
2021 FS	STL	MLB	27	600	98	.283	-0.6	SS 1	1.7
2021 DC	STL	MLB	27	594	98	.283	-0.6	SS 1	1.7

Paul DeJong, continued

Batted Ball Distribution

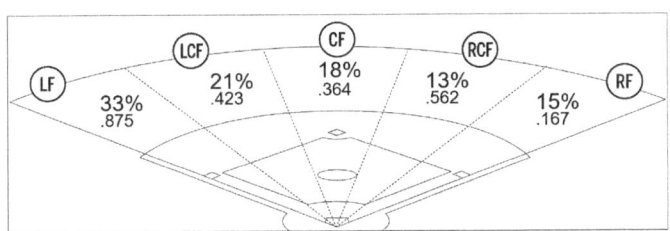

Strike Zone vs LHP   Strike Zone vs RHP

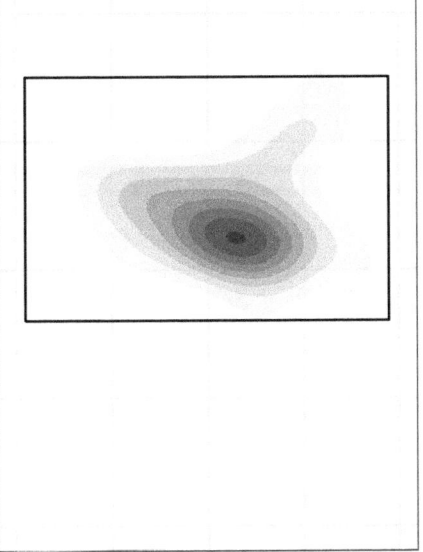

St. Louis Cardinals 2021

Tommy Edman SS
Born: 05/09/95   Age: 26   Bats: S   Throws: R
Height: 5'10"   Weight: 180   Origin: Round 6, 2016 Draft (#196 overall)

YEAR	TEAM	LVL	AGE	PA	R	2B	3B	HR	RBI	BB	K	SB	CS	AVG/OBP/SLG
2018	SPR	AA	23	498	71	23	3	6	36	35	76	27	5	.299/.350/.403
2018	MEM	AAA	23	76	13	0	1	1	5	8	11	3	0	.318/.382/.394
2019	MEM	AAA	24	218	39	12	4	7	29	15	33	9	0	.305/.356/.513
2019	STL	MLB	24	349	59	17	7	11	36	16	61	15	1	.304/.350/.500
2020	STL	MLB	25	227	29	7	1	5	26	16	48	2	4	.250/.317/.368
2021 FS	STL	MLB	26	600	76	25	4	13	54	38	126	12	3	.252/.307/.393
2021 DC	STL	MLB	26	620	78	26	5	14	56	40	130	13	3	.252/.307/.393

Comparables: Max Alvis, Wes Helms, Dave Hollins

Last summer's limited release of *The Edman Who Fell To Earth* may have been somewhat predictable and disappointing, but there was enough talent on display to expect a successful run. Smashing double-digit home runs and slugging an ultra-cool .500 during his 2019 debut was a totally alien experience for Edman, so no one should have been surprised when the fleet switch-hitter went back to his offensive roots by slapping singles, drawing the occasional walk and posting mundane numbers in line with what you should expect from him going forward. Overexposed as a headline player, Edman's speed and capable defense all around the diamond buoys his chances to carve out a long and versatile career.

YEAR	TEAM	LVL	AGE	PA	DRC+	BABIP	BRR	FRAA	WARP
2018	SPR	AA	23	498	114	.345	3.4	SS(65): -1.4, 2B(22): 1.1, 3B(22): 0.7	1.9
2018	MEM	AAA	23	76	119	.357	1.0	2B(14): 1.4, SS(3): -0.1	0.6
2019	MEM	AAA	24	218	102	.333	3.7	2B(25): 0.0, SS(10): -1.5, 3B(9): -0.5	1.1
2019	STL	MLB	24	349	109	.346	4.7	3B(55): 0.3, 2B(29): 0.7, RF(12): 1.0	2.3
2020	STL	MLB	25	227	84	.301	1.5	3B(31): 0.3, SS(13): -1.1, RF(13): -1.5	0.0
2021 FS	STL	MLB	26	600	94	.300	1.0	2B 3, SS 0	1.6
2021 DC	STL	MLB	26	620	94	.300	1.0	2B 3, SS 0	1.8

Tommy Edman, continued

Batted Ball Distribution

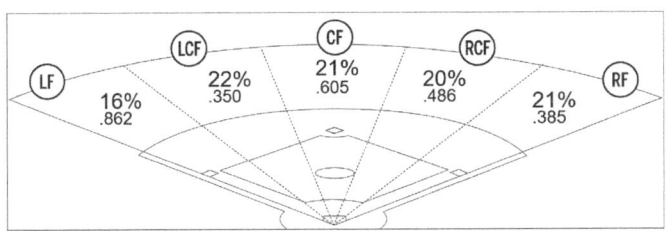

Strike Zone vs LHP   Strike Zone vs RHP

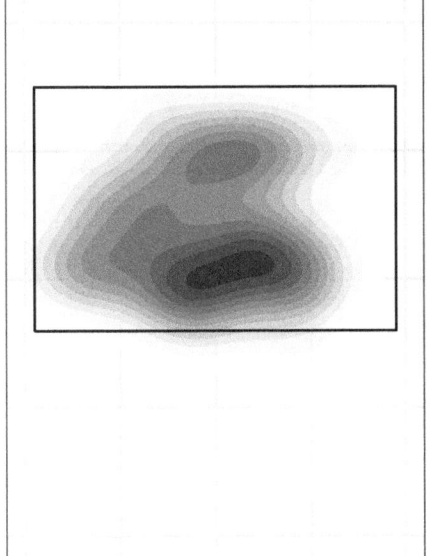

Paul Goldschmidt 1B

Born: 09/10/87   Age: 33   Bats: R   Throws: R
Height: 6'3"   Weight: 220   Origin: Round 8, 2009 Draft (#246 overall)

YEAR	TEAM	LVL	AGE	PA	R	2B	3B	HR	RBI	BB	K	SB	CS	AVG/OBP/SLG
2018	ARI	MLB	30	690	95	35	5	33	83	90	173	7	4	.290/.389/.533
2019	STL	MLB	31	682	97	25	1	34	97	78	166	3	1	.260/.346/.476
2020	STL	MLB	32	231	31	13	0	6	21	37	43	1	0	.304/.417/.466
2021 FS	STL	MLB	33	600	89	23	1	23	75	90	140	13	5	.260/.375/.454
2021 DC	STL	MLB	33	610	91	24	1	23	76	92	143	13	5	.260/.375/.454

Comparables: Fred McGriff, Harmon Killebrew, Carlos Delgado

The Cardinals signed Goldschmidt to get on base and provide power in the middle of their lineup, and he's done exactly that—just not quite both at the same time. Goldschmidt's 2019 season featured the power and run production we've grown to expect from him, but his batting average and on-base percentage were those of a mere mortal. Last year he once again reached base at an elite rate but posted by far the lowest isolated power mark of his career, sacrificing some pull-side pop in order to avoid strikeouts and stroke a few more line drives to right field. Whether he chooses the Slugger or Hitter avatar going forward he'll still be worth the $22 million he's due each of the next four seasons, but America's First Baseman is no longer tied to the .300/.400/.500 Goldy standard.

YEAR	TEAM	LVL	AGE	PA	DRC+	BABIP	BRR	FRAA	WARP
2018	ARI	MLB	30	690	136	.359	-1.3	1B(155): 1.7	4.1
2019	STL	MLB	31	682	119	.302	-0.8	1B(159): -7.3	1.9
2020	STL	MLB	32	231	126	.364	-0.7	1B(52): 2.7	1.3
2021 FS	STL	MLB	33	600	134	.313	0.2	1B 0	3.5
2021 DC	STL	MLB	33	610	134	.313	0.2	1B 0	3.6

Paul Goldschmidt, continued

Batted Ball Distribution

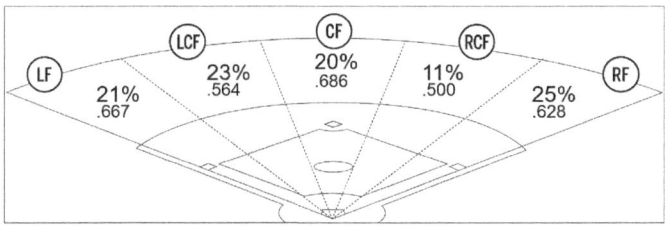

Strike Zone vs LHP   Strike Zone vs RHP

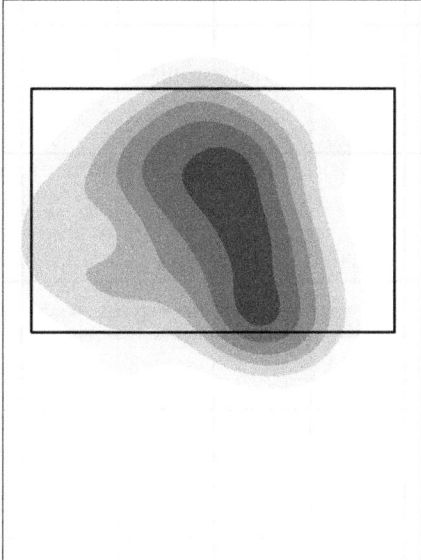

St. Louis Cardinals 2021

Yadier Molina C
Born: 07/13/82 Age: 38 Bats: R Throws: R
Height: 5'11" Weight: 225 Origin: Round 4, 2000 Draft (#113 overall)

YEAR	TEAM	LVL	AGE	PA	R	2B	3B	HR	RBI	BB	K	SB	CS	AVG/OBP/SLG
2018	STL	MLB	35	503	55	20	0	20	74	29	66	4	3	.261/.314/.436
2019	STL	MLB	36	452	45	24	0	10	57	23	58	6	0	.270/.312/.399
2020	STL	MLB	37	156	12	2	0	4	16	6	21	0	0	.262/.303/.359
2021 FS	STL	MLB	38	600	57	22	0	14	62	33	98	7	3	.247/.295/.369
2021 DC	STL	MLB	38	463	44	17	0	11	48	25	75	4	3	.247/.295/.369

Comparables: Ramon Hernandez, Mike Redmond, Carlos Ruiz

It's clear that Molina, who crossed the 2,000-hit plateau last year, is no longer quite the offensive or defensive force he once was. It's also clear that doesn't really matter at this point, that his career has soared well past any need to apply objective analysis. There's no way we can quantify how much value his game-calling skills, leadership and confidence-building influence provides to his organization, so we have to take the word of every teammate, coach, manager and opponent when they say it's immense. And that, too, no longer really matters. Willie Nelson claims that Trigger, his beat up old Martin, has the greatest tone of any guitar in the world. There's no way that's objectively true, but as long as Trigger's worn and battle-scarred body holds up and is able to produce sound, who in their right mind would argue Willie Nelson would be better playing something else?

YEAR	TEAM	P. COUNT	FRM RUNS	BLK RUNS	THRW RUNS	TOT RUNS
2018	STL	17406	2.3	1.2	0.1	3.7
2019	STL	15645	0.3	1.5	-0.1	1.8
2020	STL	5637	2.2	0.0	-0.2	2.1
2021	STL	16650	1.8	2.3	1.4	5.5
2021	STL	16650	1.8	1.5	1.4	4.7

YEAR	TEAM	LVL	AGE	PA	DRC+	BABIP	BRR	FRAA	WARP
2018	STL	MLB	35	503	110	.264	-2.3	C(121): 1.4, 1B(5): 0.0	3.1
2019	STL	MLB	36	452	91	.289	-2.4	C(111): 0.6, 1B(4): 0.0, 3B(1): -0.0	1.7
2020	STL	MLB	37	156	91	.281	-1.0	C(42): -0.2, 1B(2): -0.0	0.5
2021 FS	STL	MLB	38	600	83	.274	-0.3	C 4, 1B 0	1.6
2021 DC	STL	MLB	38	463	83	.274	-0.2	C 4	1.3

Yadier Molina, continued

Batted Ball Distribution

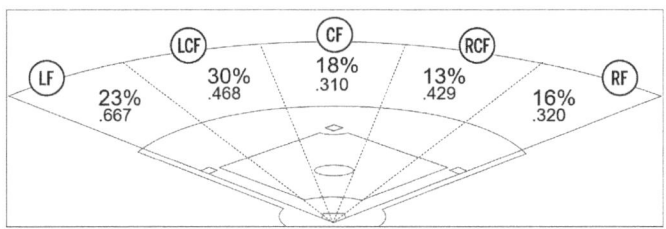

Strike Zone vs LHP   Strike Zone vs RHP

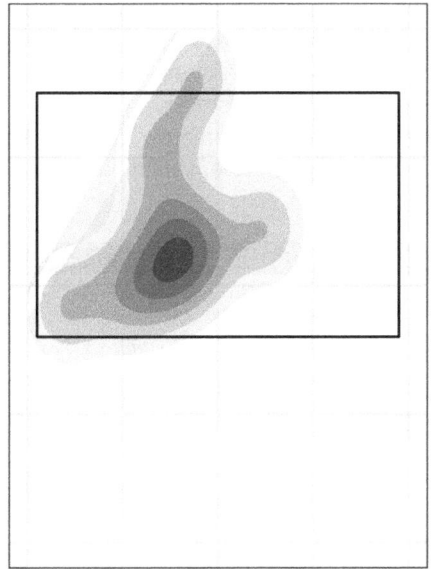 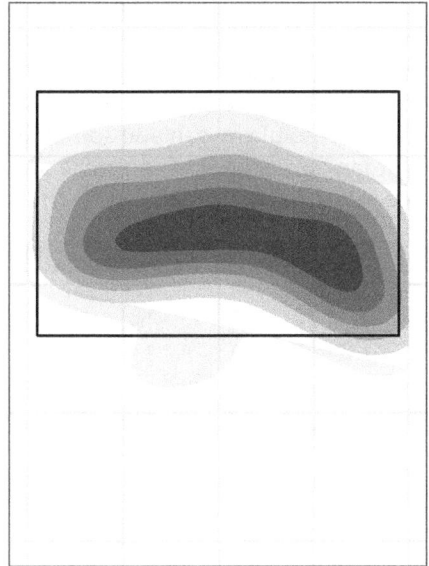

Tyler O'Neill LF

Born: 06/22/95   Age: 26   Bats: R   Throws: R
Height: 5'11"   Weight: 200   Origin: Round 3, 2013 Draft (#85 overall)

YEAR	TEAM	LVL	AGE	PA	R	2B	3B	HR	RBI	BB	K	SB	CS	AVG/OBP/SLG
2018	MEM	AAA	23	273	61	9	2	26	63	29	68	3	1	.311/.385/.693
2018	STL	MLB	23	142	29	5	0	9	23	7	57	2	0	.254/.303/.500
2019	MEM	AAA	24	166	26	5	0	11	26	14	51	3	0	.265/.325/.517
2019	STL	MLB	24	151	18	6	0	5	16	10	53	1	0	.262/.311/.411
2020	STL	MLB	25	157	20	5	0	7	19	15	43	3	1	.173/.261/.360
2021 FS	STL	MLB	26	600	74	23	1	27	81	54	195	1	1	.225/.301/.429
2021 DC	STL	MLB	26	461	57	17	1	20	62	41	150	0	1	.225/.301/.429

Comparables: Billy Ashley, Bo Jackson, Pete Incaviglia

First, the good news: O'Neill walked more, struck out less and began to take advantage of his blazing speed and natural athleticism to play a tremendous, Gold Glove-winning left field last year. His swinging strike rate was no longer among the worst in the league, and it wasn't even extraordinarily awful. However, more frequent contact came at the expense of his calling card: power. O'Neill simply stopped hitting the ball hard, posting a .187 isolated power score that barely exceeds sluggers like Freddy Galvis and José Iglesias and a league-low batting average on balls in play. His exit velocity last year was in the 36th percentile. Now that O'Neill has worked to regain some mastery of the strike zone it's possible he can add some thunder back into his swing, but that's easier said than done. Any fool can solve one side of a Rubik's Cube; solving all six at once is the real trick.

YEAR	TEAM	LVL	AGE	PA	DRC+	BABIP	BRR	FRAA	WARP
2018	MEM	AAA	23	273	162	.324	1.0	LF(33): -1.3, RF(21): 7.8, CF(6): -1.0	2.9
2018	STL	MLB	23	142	89	.364	2.2	RF(24): 0.7, LF(16): 1.1, CF(3): -0.4	0.5
2019	MEM	AAA	24	166	104	.322	0.7	LF(25): 0.2, RF(11): 1.0	0.6
2019	STL	MLB	24	151	75	.386	-0.9	LF(33): -3.3, RF(8): -0.2, CF(3): 0.3	-0.4
2020	STL	MLB	25	157	95	.189	-0.6	LF(48): 8.4	0.9
2021 FS	STL	MLB	26	600	103	.293	-0.7	LF 0, CF 0	1.7
2021 DC	STL	MLB	26	461	103	.293	-0.5	LF 0	1.3

Tyler O'Neill, continued

Batted Ball Distribution

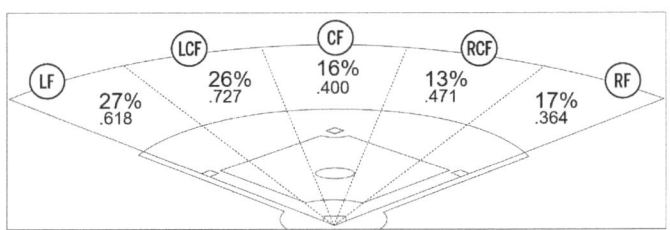

Strike Zone vs LHP   Strike Zone vs RHP

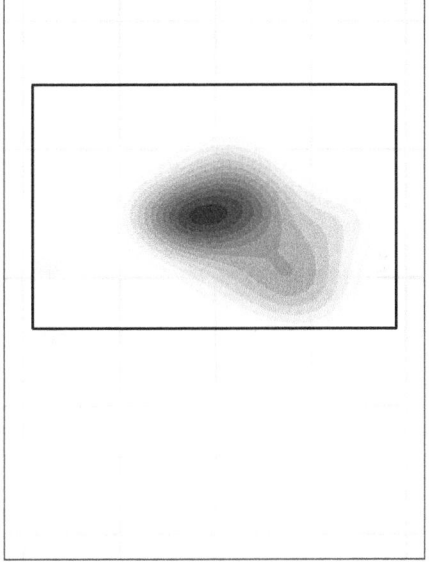

Génesis Cabrera LHP

Born: 10/10/96 Age: 24 Bats: L Throws: L
Height: 6'2" Weight: 180 Origin: International Free Agent, 2013

YEAR	TEAM	LVL	AGE	W	L	SV	G	GS	IP	H	HR	BB/9	K/9	K	GB%	BABIP
2018	MTG	AA	21	7	6	0	21	20	113^2	90	11	4.5	9.8	124	34.7%	.282
2018	SPR	AA	21	1	3	0	5	5	24^2	24	3	4.7	7.7	21	34.2%	.300
2019	MEM	AAA	22	5	6	0	20	18	99	107	20	3.5	9.6	106	39.8%	.333
2019	STL	MLB	22	0	2	1	13	2	20^1	23	2	4.9	8.4	19	37.3%	.328
2020	STL	MLB	23	4	1	1	19	0	22^1	10	3	6.4	12.9	32	34.1%	.171
2021 FS	STL	MLB	24	2	3	0	57	0	50	44	7	5.1	9.9	55	36.8%	.288
2021 DC	STL	MLB	24	2	2	0	50	0	52.7	47	7	5.1	9.9	58	36.8%	.288

Comparables: Beau Burrows, Justus Sheffield, Caleb Ferguson

There was a time not so long ago, a time when phones plugged into walls, maps lived in glove compartments and fictional TV presidents disarmed opponents with logic, during which Cabrera's crackling lefty heat would have made him a unicorn. In today's game his velo isn't even in the top 10 percent, but, when you combine it with two effective secondaries and a flailing, Carlos Marmol-like delivery, you can see why he generates swinging strikes at an elite rate. Like Marmol, fewer than half of the batters Cabrera faced last year managed to put the ball in play; and, also like Marmol, Cabrera's lack of command and control can produce flurries of walks, plunks, wild pitches, gopher balls and self-inflicted rallies. Few mid-20s fireballers ever fully cure their wildness, so Cabrera's future likely lies in high-leverage relief (though, once more like Marmol, he'll be a leading cause of managerial hypertension if allowed to work the ninth).

YEAR	TEAM	LVL	AGE	WHIP	ERA	DRA-	WARP	MPH	FB%	WHF	CSP
2018	MTG	AA	21	1.29	4.12	109	0.2				
2018	SPR	AA	21	1.50	4.74	104	0.0				
2019	MEM	AAA	22	1.47	5.91	105	1.5				
2019	STL	MLB	22	1.67	4.87	113	0.0	98.3	61.0%	18.1%	
2020	STL	MLB	23	1.16	2.42	90	0.3	98.2	56.4%	40.3%	
2021 FS	STL	MLB	24	1.46	4.62	105	0.1	98.3	58.2%	31.7%	47.4%
2021 DC	STL	MLB	24	1.46	4.62	105	0.1	98.3	58.2%	31.7%	47.4%

Génesis Cabrera, continued

Pitch Shape vs LHH

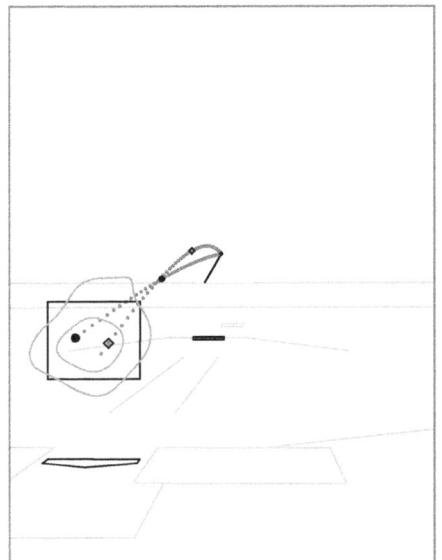

Pitch Shape vs RHH

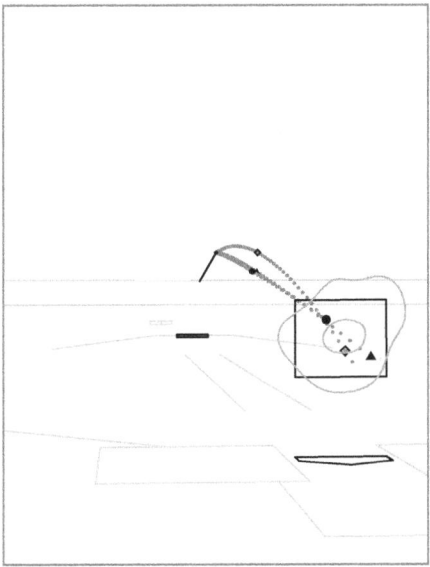

Type	Frequency	Velocity	H Movement	V Movement
● Fastball	50.6%	96.4 [112]	7.2 [98]	-10.2 [114]
☐ Sinker	5.8%	96.4 [121]	12.3 [106]	-13.4 [123]
▲ Changeup	13.1%	88.7 [114]	12.6 [95]	-21.5 [117]
◇ Curveball	30.5%	81.6 [111]	-6.1 [94]	-46.7 [104]

Seth Elledge RHP

Born: 05/20/96   Age: 25   Bats: R   Throws: R
Height: 6'3"   Weight: 240   Origin: Round 4, 2017 Draft (#123 overall)

YEAR	TEAM	LVL	AGE	W	L	SV	G	GS	IP	H	HR	BB/9	K/9	K	GB%	BABIP
2018	MOD	HI-A	22	5	1	9	31	0	38[1]	18	1	3.5	12.7	54	46.2%	.224
2018	SPR	AA	22	3	1	4	13	0	16[2]	13	3	3.2	10.8	20	37.2%	.270
2019	SPR	AA	23	3	3	3	26	0	33[1]	34	3	3.5	11.6	43	42.9%	.388
2019	MEM	AAA	23	3	1	0	21	3	34[1]	28	3	5.0	8.4	32	38.0%	.284
2020	STL	MLB	24	1	0	0	12	0	11[2]	11	2	6.2	10.8	14	39.3%	.346
2021 FS	STL	MLB	25	2	2	0	57	0	50	43	7	4.6	10.0	55	40.0%	.284
2021 DC	STL	MLB	25	1	1	0	28	0	35	30	5	4.6	10.0	39	40.0%	.284

Comparables: Sammy Gervacio, Steven Okert, Jacob Rhame

When you take the already small sample of a single reliever season, apply the COVID-19 reduction, apply the rookie factor and carve off a platoon split, there's good reason not to make too much of Elledge's struggles against lefties last year. On the other hand, a 1.300 OPS draws the eye and is exactly the concern that always exists for a two-pitch reliever like Elledge. The young Texan doesn't have eye-popping stuff but he misses bats and his inflated walk rate last season doesn't align with his solid minor-league numbers. Elledge should be able to scratch out a career in middle relief, but he'll need to be spotted carefully unless he can find some voodoo to tame portside hitters.

YEAR	TEAM	LVL	AGE	WHIP	ERA	DRA-	WARP	MPH	FB%	WHF	CSP
2018	MOD	HI-A	22	0.86	1.17	63	0.8				
2018	SPR	AA	22	1.14	4.32	47	0.5				
2019	SPR	AA	23	1.41	3.78	107	-0.3				
2019	MEM	AAA	23	1.37	4.72	98	0.5				
2020	STL	MLB	24	1.63	4.63	95	0.1	94.9	64.9%	27.9%	
2021 FS	STL	MLB	25	1.38	4.22	98	0.3	94.9	64.9%	27.9%	43.5%
2021 DC	STL	MLB	25	1.38	4.22	98	0.2	94.9	64.9%	27.9%	43.5%

Seth Elledge, continued

Pitch Shape vs LHH

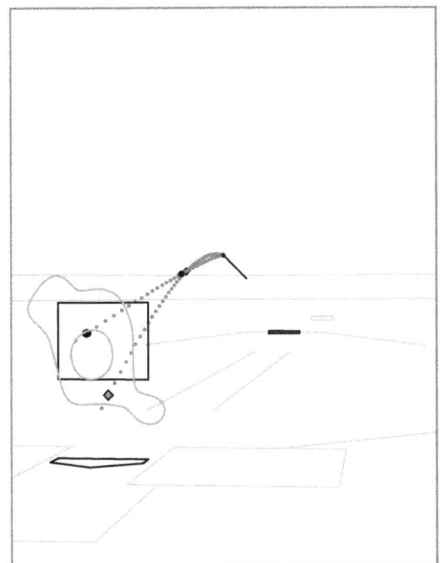

Pitch Shape vs RHH

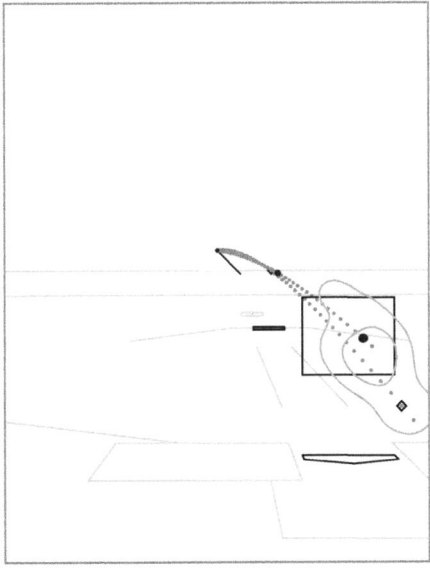

Type	Frequency	Velocity	H Movement	V Movement
● Fastball	64.7%	93.5 [103]	-11.5 [77]	-14.9 [101]
◇ Curveball	34.9%	83.4 [119]	2.9 [81]	-41.6 [115]

St. Louis Cardinals 2021

Jack Flaherty   RHP

Born: 10/15/95   Age: 25   Bats: R   Throws: R
Height: 6'4"   Weight: 225   Origin: Round 1, 2014 Draft (#34 overall)

YEAR	TEAM	LVL	AGE	W	L	SV	G	GS	IP	H	HR	BB/9	K/9	K	GB%	BABIP
2018	MEM	AAA	22	4	1	0	5	5	31^2	22	2	2.0	11.7	41	44.0%	.274
2018	STL	MLB	22	8	9	0	29	29	158	109	21	3.5	11.1	195	42.1%	.252
2019	STL	MLB	23	11	8	0	33	33	196^1	135	25	2.5	10.6	231	39.7%	.244
2020	STL	MLB	24	4	3	0	9	9	40^1	33	6	3.6	10.9	49	44.1%	.284
2021 FS	STL	MLB	25	10	7	0	26	26	150	121	18	3.4	10.7	178	41.7%	.282
2021 DC	STL	MLB	25	11	8	0	29	29	172	139	21	3.4	10.7	204	41.7%	.282

Comparables: Luis Severino, Lance McCullers Jr., Yovani Gallardo

First, some perspective.

Over 9 starts during April and May of 2019, with no designated hitter, Jacob deGrom posted a 4.68 ERA, allowing a .744 OPS. Over the full season, deGrom posted a 2.43 ERA and allowed a .565 OPS. He won the Cy Young Award.

Over eight of his nine starts last season, with the designated hitter, Flaherty pitched to a 3.13 ERA and allowed a .582 OPS. In his other start, the Brewers lit into him for nine runs over three innings. Over the full season, Flaherty posted a 4.91 ERA and allowed a .677 OPS. Some considered him a disappointment.

That Milwaukee faceplant happened, but the limitations of short-season plague ball didn't allow Flaherty enough innings to wash it clean. He allowed a few more walks and home runs than normal, but his strikeout rate remained elite. He has estimable command and his wide repertoire, especially that disappearing slider, can be fearsome. Flaherty is 25 years old, healthy, and under team control for 3 more seasons.

He is who you thought he was.

YEAR	TEAM	LVL	AGE	WHIP	ERA	DRA-	WARP	MPH	FB%	WHF	CSP
2018	MEM	AAA	22	0.92	2.27	35	1.4				
2018	STL	MLB	22	1.08	3.25	68	3.9	95.6	55.3%	31.6%	
2019	STL	MLB	23	0.97	2.75	50	7.1	96.5	57.7%	30.9%	
2020	STL	MLB	24	1.21	4.91	85	0.7	96.2	55.6%	34.5%	
2021 FS	STL	MLB	25	1.19	3.22	79	3.2	96.2	56.7%	31.7%	46.0%
2021 DC	STL	MLB	25	1.19	3.22	79	3.7	96.2	56.7%	31.7%	46.0%

Jack Flaherty, continued

Pitch Shape vs LHH

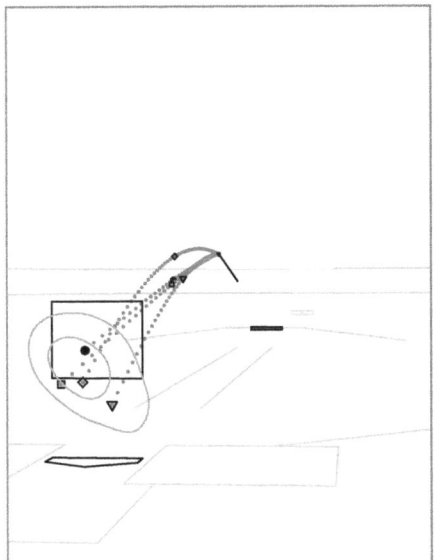

Pitch Shape vs RHH

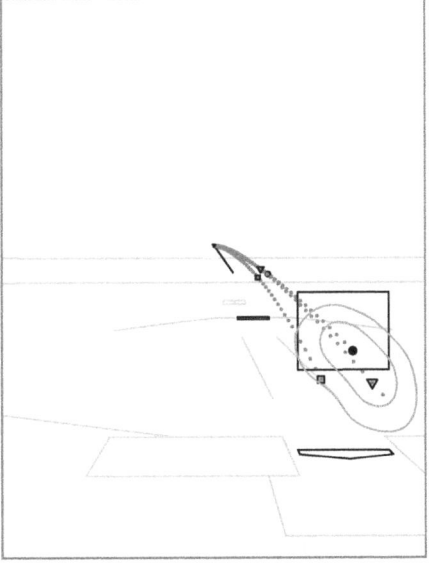

Type	Frequency	Velocity	H Movement	V Movement
● Fastball	44.2%	94.2 [105]	-5.2 [107]	-14.2 [103]
☐ Sinker	11.4%	92.3 [99]	-10.7 [117]	-21.4 [97]
▽ Slider	28.7%	84.7 [103]	5.6 [101]	-31.5 [107]
◇ Curveball	13.6%	77.6 [96]	11.4 [116]	-51.9 [92]

Giovanny Gallegos RHP

Born: 08/14/91   Age: 29   Bats: R   Throws: R
Height: 6'2"   Weight: 215   Origin: International Free Agent, 2011

YEAR	TEAM	LVL	AGE	W	L	SV	G	GS	IP	H	HR	BB/9	K/9	K	GB%	BABIP
2018	SWB	AAA	26	2	1	2	17	0	27^2	24	1	2.3	13.3	41	36.4%	.365
2018	MEM	AAA	26	0	0	1	13	0	16^2	7	0	1.6	8.6	16	42.5%	.179
2018	NYY	MLB	26	0	0	1	4	0	10	10	2	2.7	9.0	10	37.0%	.333
2018	STL	MLB	26	0	0	0	2	0	1^1	1	0	0.0	13.5	2	0.0%	.333
2019	STL	MLB	27	3	2	1	66	0	74	44	9	1.9	11.3	93	33.5%	.222
2020	STL	MLB	28	2	2	4	16	0	15	9	1	2.4	12.6	21	40.6%	.258
2021 FS	STL	MLB	29	3	2	24	57	0	50	38	6	2.4	11.6	64	36.1%	.274
2021 DC	STL	MLB	29	2	2	24	50	0	52.7	40	7	2.4	11.6	67	36.1%	.274

Comparables: Dominic Leone, Nick Wittgren, Ryan Dull

Gallegos worked with his usual grit and determination last year, overcoming an undisclosed euphemism in July and a groin pull in September to post another solid season in the Cardinals bullpen. His high-spin fastball isn't explosive but Gallegos commands it well and his breaker is pure kryptonite. He calls it a slider even though it has 12-6 break like a curve and can fall off the table in a manner that would make Bruce Sutter smile with fond remembrance. Gallegos is no spring chicken, having kicked around the Yankees organization for years before finally getting a chance in St Louis to unleash his slide-piece on an unready world, but he's a good bet to spend his 30s troubling the sleep of big-league hitters.

YEAR	TEAM	LVL	AGE	WHIP	ERA	DRA-	WARP	MPH	FB%	WHF	CSP
2018	SWB	AAA	26	1.12	3.90	46	0.9				
2018	MEM	AAA	26	0.60	0.54	54	0.5				
2018	NYY	MLB	26	1.30	4.50	120	-0.1	95.3	58.6%	18.2%	
2018	STL	MLB	26	0.75	0.00	152	0.0	95.9	64.0%	16.7%	
2019	STL	MLB	27	0.81	2.31	57	2.0	94.9	55.2%	34.7%	
2020	STL	MLB	28	0.87	3.60	76	0.3	95.7	48.9%	38.1%	
2021 FS	STL	MLB	29	1.03	2.57	67	1.2	95.1	54.1%	34.4%	46.8%
2021 DC	STL	MLB	29	1.03	2.57	67	1.2	95.1	54.1%	34.4%	46.8%

Giovanny Gallegos, continued

Pitch Shape vs LHH

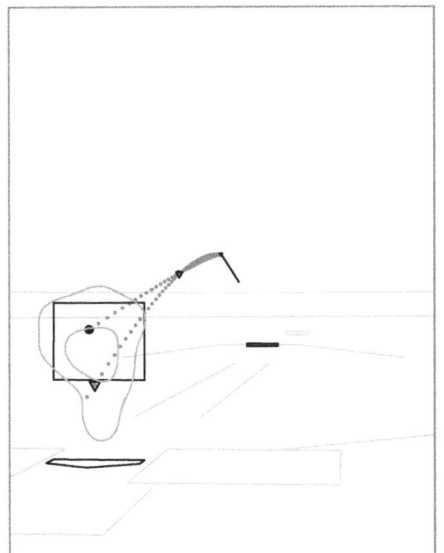

Pitch Shape vs RHH

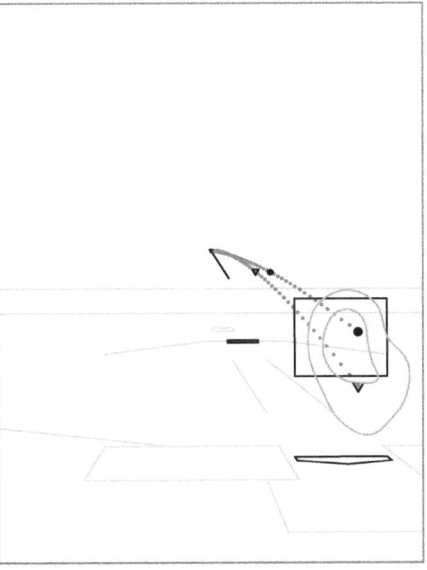

Type	Frequency	Velocity	H Movement	V Movement
● Fastball	48.5%	93.9 [104]	-8.8 [90]	-12.5 [108]
▽ Slider	50.7%	85.6 [107]	2 [88]	-33.3 [101]

Ryan Helsley RHP

Born: 07/18/94 Age: 26 Bats: R Throws: R
Height: 6'2" Weight: 230 Origin: Round 5, 2015 Draft (#161 overall)

YEAR	TEAM	LVL	AGE	W	L	SV	G	GS	IP	H	HR	BB/9	K/9	K	GB%	BABIP
2018	SPR	AA	23	3	2	0	7	7	41	30	5	4.4	9.7	44	45.4%	.253
2018	MEM	AAA	23	2	1	0	5	5	26²	18	2	3.0	11.5	34	36.5%	.267
2019	MEM	AAA	24	2	3	1	17	7	37¹	29	3	4.8	9.9	41	41.5%	.289
2019	STL	MLB	24	2	0	0	24	0	36²	34	5	2.9	7.9	32	33.0%	.282
2020	STL	MLB	25	1	1	1	12	0	12	8	3	6.0	7.5	10	33.3%	.167
2021 FS	STL	MLB	26	2	2	0	57	0	50	45	8	4.3	9.1	50	37.9%	.280
2021 DC	STL	MLB	26	2	2	0	50	0	52.7	48	8	4.3	9.1	53	37.9%	.280

Comparables: Drew Anderson, Alex Reyes, Antonio Bastardo

Jordan Hicks' absence and Carlos Martínez's intended return to the rotation provided Helsley a chance last summer to move up the bullpen pecking order and perhaps audition for the closer role. Unfortunately the young Oklahoman contracted COVID-19, missed the whole of August and never seemed to find his control or his rhythm when he returned. At his best Helsley can command his rising high-90s heat and produce plenty of empty swings with his sharp cutter and power curve, a broad enough repertoire for a starting role but with a few too many walks sprinkled in. Helsley has the stuff, makeup and moxie to thrive in the late innings, and if normal ever returns he has a shot to someday make the ninth his workplace.

YEAR	TEAM	LVL	AGE	WHIP	ERA	DRA-	WARP	MPH	FB%	WHF	CSP
2018	SPR	AA	23	1.22	4.39	67	1.0				
2018	MEM	AAA	23	1.01	3.71	51	0.9				
2019	MEM	AAA	24	1.31	4.58	63	1.2				
2019	STL	MLB	24	1.25	2.95	103	0.1	100.1	56.6%	22.3%	
2020	STL	MLB	25	1.33	5.25	139	-0.1	99.2	43.3%	31.9%	
2021 FS	STL	MLB	26	1.39	4.38	103	0.2	99.8	52.1%	25.5%	50.4%
2021 DC	STL	MLB	26	1.39	4.38	103	0.2	99.8	52.1%	25.5%	50.4%

Ryan Helsley, continued

Pitch Shape vs LHH

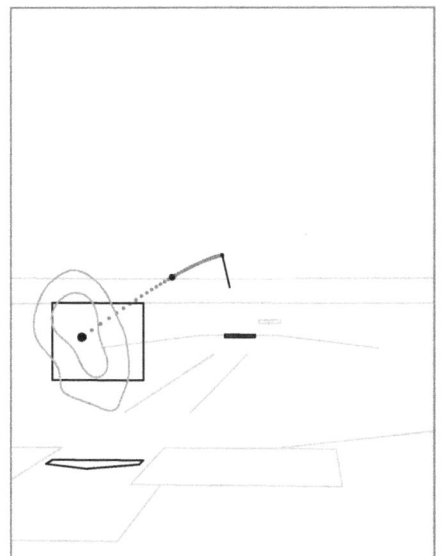

Pitch Shape vs RHH

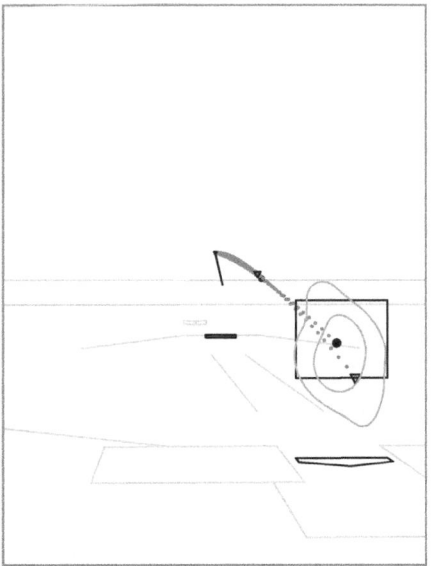

Type	Frequency	Velocity	H Movement	V Movement
● Fastball	42.4%	97.2 [115]	-2.9 [118]	-12 [109]
▲ Changeup	4.0%	89.6 [117]	-12.5 [96]	-20.9 [118]
▽ Slider	34.8%	87.5 [116]	3.9 [95]	-30 [111]
◇ Curveball	16.7%	80.8 [108]	3.4 [83]	-48.5 [100]

Dakota Hudson RHP

Born: 09/15/94   Age: 26   Bats: R   Throws: R
Height: 6'5"   Weight: 215   Origin: Round 1, 2016 Draft (#34 overall)

YEAR	TEAM	LVL	AGE	W	L	SV	G	GS	IP	H	HR	BB/9	K/9	K	GB%	BABIP
2018	MEM	AAA	23	13	3	0	19	19	111^2	107	1	3.1	7.0	87	57.6%	.315
2018	STL	MLB	23	4	1	0	26	0	27^1	19	0	5.9	6.3	19	62.5%	.237
2019	STL	MLB	24	16	7	1	33	32	174^2	160	22	4.4	7.0	136	56.3%	.275
2020	STL	MLB	25	3	2	0	8	8	39	24	5	3.5	7.2	31	57.7%	.192
2021 FS	STL	MLB	26	2	2	0	57	0	50	46	5	4.3	7.8	43	55.5%	.283

Comparables: Antonio Senzatela, Dana Eveland, Brad Hand

Hudson was sidelined after eight starts last summer and underwent Tommy John surgery, which is unfortunate in a lot of ways. It deprives Hudson of the chance to compete at the game he loves and build towards a higher salary; it deprives the Cardinals of a potential mid-rotation cog; and it deprives analysts of the opportunity to see if Hudson can continue to out-pitch his peripherals. It's not a mystery how he's keeping runs off the board despite sub-par walk and strikeout rates and plenty of hard contact: lots of groundballs coupled with a low batting average on balls in play and a high strand rate. But ground balls tend to lead to more hits, not fewer, so you'd expect a lot more of those hard-hit grounders to turn into singles over time. Hasn't happened yet, though, and with Hudson likely missing most of the coming year we'll have to wait a while to see if he can keep thumbing his nose at expectations.

YEAR	TEAM	LVL	AGE	WHIP	ERA	DRA-	WARP	MPH	FB%	WHF	CSP
2018	MEM	AAA	23	1.30	2.50	75	2.6				
2018	STL	MLB	23	1.35	2.63	143	-0.5	97.4	60.7%	22.9%	
2019	STL	MLB	24	1.41	3.35	92	2.4	95.4	61.7%	23.8%	
2020	STL	MLB	25	1.00	2.77	88	0.6	94.8	58.6%	21.9%	
2021 FS	STL	MLB	26	1.41	4.27	99	0.3	95.4	61.0%	23.3%	45.8%

Dakota Hudson, continued

Pitch Shape vs LHH

Pitch Shape vs RHH

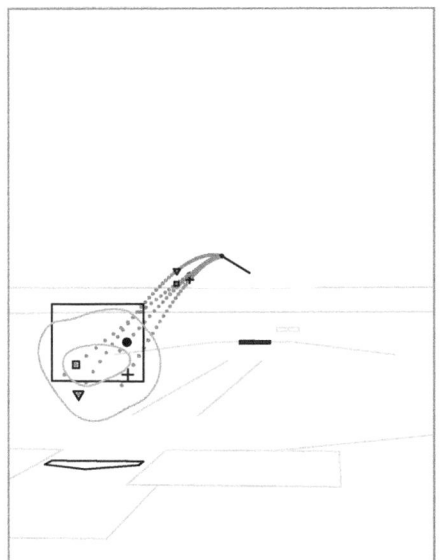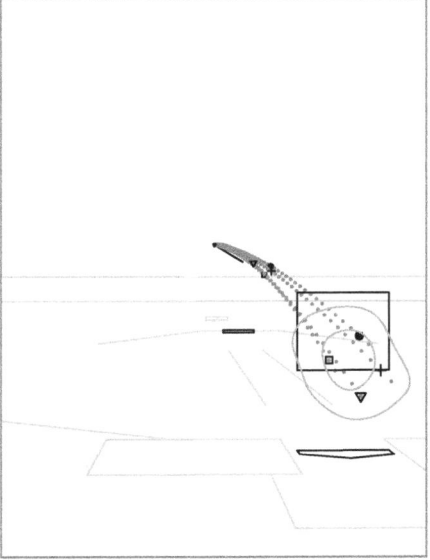

Type	Frequency	Velocity	H Movement	V Movement
● Fastball	22.2%	92.9 [101]	-4.6 [110]	-19.4 [88]
□ Sinker	36.3%	93.3 [104]	-12.8 [102]	-18.6 [106]
+ Cutter	20.7%	88.8 [103]	-0.3 [85]	-25.9 [93]
▽ Slider	18.6%	82.4 [93]	5 [99]	-39.4 [84]

St. Louis Cardinals 2021

Kwang Hyun Kim   LHP
Born: 07/22/88   Age: 32   Bats: L   Throws: L
Height: 6'2"   Weight: 195   Origin: International Free Agent, 2019

YEAR	TEAM	LVL	AGE	W	L	SV	G	GS	IP	H	HR	BB/9	K/9	K	GB%	BABIP
2020	STL	MLB	31	3	0	1	8	7	39	28	3	2.8	5.5	24	50.0%	.217
2021 FS	STL	MLB	32	9	8	0	26	26	150	146	19	3.2	7.3	122	47.1%	.285
2021 DC	STL	MLB	32	9	8	0	25	25	139.7	136	18	3.2	7.3	114	47.1%	.285

After 11 successful seasons in the KBO with the SK Wyverns, Kim negotiated a global pandemic, unexpected isolation from his family, a kidney ailment and an organization committed to using him in the bullpen to eventually succeed in a big-league rotation. Wyverns are mythical creatures that look like dragons, but walk on two legs and don't breathe fire. Similarly, Kim doesn't breathe fire but succeeds by working the bottom of the zone with his low-velo fastball and a wide assortment of offspeed junk that keeps hitters from timing him up. There's very little swing-and-miss but lots of routine ground balls and since Kim doesn't walk anyone that's been enough so far to keep runs off the board. It's hard to consistently succeed in today's game while allowing that much contact, so Kim's novelty is likely to fade and big-league hitters will figure him out soon enough.

YEAR	TEAM	LVL	AGE	WHIP	ERA	DRA-	WARP	MPH	FB%	WHF	CSP
2020	STL	MLB	31	1.03	1.62	116	0.0	92.2	48.3%	18.3%	
2021 FS	STL	MLB	32	1.34	4.03	96	1.8	92.2	48.3%	18.3%	48.6%
2021 DC	STL	MLB	32	1.34	4.03	96	1.6	92.2	48.3%	18.3%	48.6%

Kwang Hyun Kim, continued

Pitch Shape vs LHH

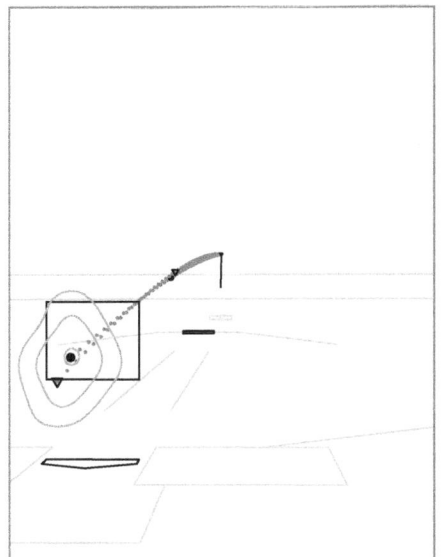

Pitch Shape vs RHH

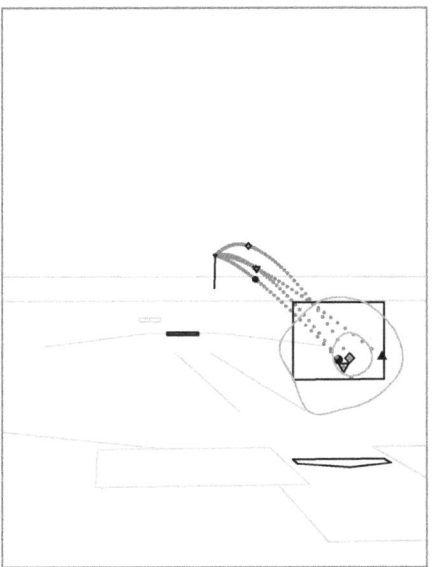

Type	Frequency	Velocity	H Movement	V Movement
● Fastball	48.0%	90.1 [92]	0.2 [131]	-16.3 [97]
▲ Changeup	8.4%	80.5 [82]	9.3 [113]	-25.6 [105]
▽ Slider	31.8%	83.3 [97]	-4.7 [98]	-32.6 [103]
◇ Curveball	11.2%	70.4 [68]	-4.8 [89]	-56.4 [82]

St. Louis Cardinals 2021

Carlos Martínez   RHP
Born: 09/21/91   Age: 29   Bats: R   Throws: R
Height: 6'0"   Weight: 200   Origin: International Free Agent, 2009

YEAR	TEAM	LVL	AGE	W	L	SV	G	GS	IP	H	HR	BB/9	K/9	K	GB%	BABIP
2018	SPR	AA	26	0	0	0	3	1	7	6	3	0.0	7.7	6	28.6%	.167
2018	STL	MLB	26	8	6	5	33	18	118²	100	5	4.6	8.9	117	48.6%	.296
2019	STL	MLB	27	4	2	24	48	0	48¹	39	2	3.4	9.9	53	57.1%	.301
2020	STL	MLB	28	0	3	0	5	5	20	32	6	4.5	7.7	17	51.3%	.371
2021 FS	STL	MLB	29	9	8	0	26	26	150	139	15	3.8	8.7	145	51.6%	.295
2021 DC	STL	MLB	29	7	6	0	21	22	120	111	12	3.8	8.7	116	51.6%	.295

Comparables: Michael Wacha, Tom Gordon, Mike Foltynewicz

It was a lost season for Martínez, who entered the season with high hopes of reclaiming a spot in the Cardinals rotation but was shelled in his first start before COVID-19 laid him low. One of the few players to cop to being hospitalized by the virus, when Martínez returned his fastball had lost three clicks and he couldn't get anyone out. He has a deep and effective arsenal, a history of success as both a starter and a closer and the only blemishes on his track record are from when he was injured or ill. On the other hand, Martinez's diminished velocity is concerning and he hasn't been truly healthy since 2017. The best choice heading forward may be to stick him back in the 'pen and see if he can sit in the mid-90s in short stints without breaking down.

YEAR	TEAM	LVL	AGE	WHIP	ERA	DRA-	WARP	MPH	FB%	WHF	CSP
2018	SPR	AA	26	0.86	3.86	74	0.1				
2018	STL	MLB	26	1.35	3.11	103	0.9	97.2	44.2%	25.1%	
2019	STL	MLB	27	1.18	3.17	67	1.1	98.3	51.0%	28.5%	
2020	STL	MLB	28	2.10	9.90	117	0.0	95.6	50.2%	19.7%	
2021 FS	STL	MLB	29	1.36	3.94	93	2.0	97.2	48.0%	24.8%	47.1%
2021 DC	STL	MLB	29	1.36	3.94	93	1.5	97.2	48.0%	24.8%	47.1%

Carlos Martínez, continued

Pitch Shape vs LHH

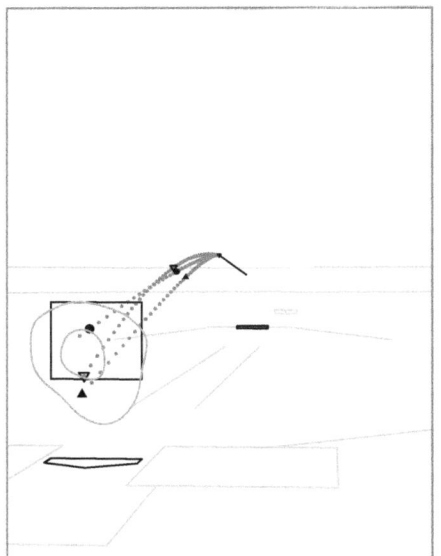

Pitch Shape vs RHH

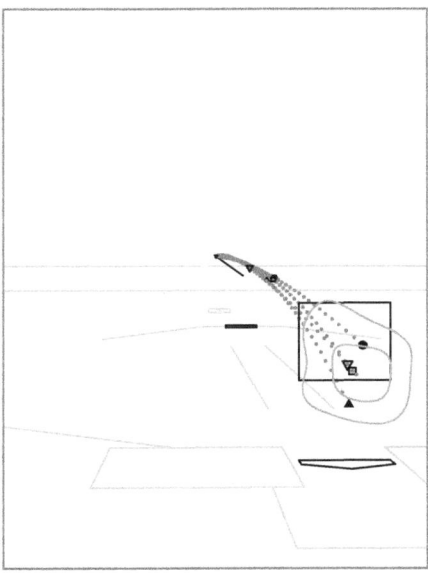

Type	Frequency	Velocity	H Movement	V Movement
● Fastball	34.7%	93.6 [103]	-7.3 [97]	-16.5 [96]
□ Sinker	14.4%	92 [98]	-14.3 [91]	-24.7 [87]
▲ Changeup	20.0%	86 [103]	-14.3 [86]	-33.9 [82]
▽ Slider	27.4%	82.9 [95]	10.6 [120]	-34.6 [98]

Andrew Miller LHP

Born: 05/21/85   Age: 36   Bats: L   Throws: L
Height: 6'7"   Weight: 200   Origin: Round 1, 2006 Draft (#6 overall)

YEAR	TEAM	LVL	AGE	W	L	SV	G	GS	IP	H	HR	BB/9	K/9	K	GB%	BABIP
2018	CLE	MLB	33	2	4	2	37	0	34	31	3	4.2	11.9	45	47.7%	.329
2019	STL	MLB	34	5	6	6	73	0	54²	45	11	4.4	11.5	70	36.6%	.283
2020	STL	MLB	35	1	1	4	16	0	13	9	0	3.5	11.1	16	61.3%	.290
2021 FS	STL	MLB	36	2	2	1	57	0	50	42	5	3.8	10.8	60	44.9%	.297
2021 DC	STL	MLB	36	2	2	1	50	0	52.7	45	6	3.8	10.8	63	44.9%	.297

Comparables: Tyler Clippard, Pedro Strop, Ian Kennedy

Miller lost two more ticks of velocity last season but his slider was still hell on wheels, especially against his fellow Leftorium patrons who went 3-for-29 facing him, all singles. The old dog even added a new trick, unveiling a sinker that helped him post the highest groundball rate of his career with nary a gopher ball to be seen. Miller's option year vested down the stretch, and while he's no longer Andrew Friggin' Miller he remains an above-average reliever who misses enough bats to be worth his final eight-figure paycheck.

YEAR	TEAM	LVL	AGE	WHIP	ERA	DRA-	WARP	MPH	FB%	WHF	CSP
2018	CLE	MLB	33	1.38	4.24	68	0.7	95.6	43.3%	31.0%	
2019	STL	MLB	34	1.32	4.45	76	1.0	95.2	38.6%	30.8%	
2020	STL	MLB	35	1.08	2.77	75	0.3	93.3	40.0%	31.4%	
2021 FS	STL	MLB	36	1.27	3.72	88	0.6	94.9	39.7%	31.0%	48.6%
2021 DC	STL	MLB	36	1.27	3.72	88	0.6	94.9	39.7%	31.0%	48.6%

Andrew Miller, continued

Pitch Shape vs LHH

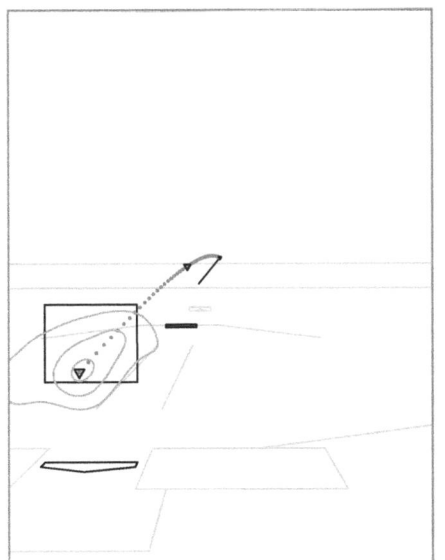

Pitch Shape vs RHH

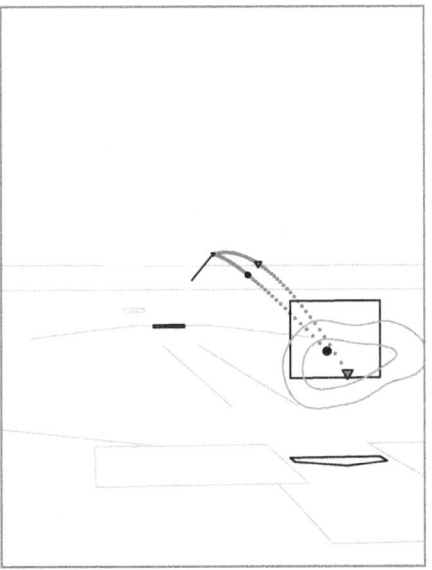

Type	Frequency	Velocity	H Movement	V Movement
● Fastball	31.1%	89.9 [91]	4.9 [109]	-18.1 [92]
☐ Sinker	8.7%	92.7 [101]	14.5 [89]	-22 [95]
▽ Slider	59.7%	80.3 [84]	-11.3 [123]	-38.1 [87]

Johan Oviedo RHP

Born: 03/02/98 Age: 23 Bats: R Throws: R
Height: 6'5" Weight: 245 Origin: International Free Agent, 2016

YEAR	TEAM	LVL	AGE	W	L	SV	G	GS	IP	H	HR	BB/9	K/9	K	GB%	BABIP
2018	PEO	LO-A	20	10	10	1	25	23	121^2	108	6	5.8	8.7	118	36.5%	.304
2019	PMB	HI-A	21	5	0	0	6	5	33^2	29	1	3.2	9.4	35	46.7%	.308
2019	SPR	AA	21	7	8	0	23	23	113	120	9	5.1	10.2	128	42.0%	.368
2020	STL	MLB	22	0	3	0	5	5	24^2	24	3	3.6	5.8	16	40.7%	.269
2021 FS	STL	MLB	23	8	10	0	26	26	150	151	24	5.1	7.8	130	40.6%	.291
2021 DC	STL	MLB	23	4	5	0	22	12	68.7	69	11	5.1	7.8	59	40.6%	.291

Comparables: Rony García, Touki Toussaint, Huascar Ynoa

The Cardinals' COVID nightmare last summer forced them to toss a few talented but unprepared young arms to the wolves, and Oviedo was among them. He's a Bunyanesque figure on the mound who can unleash mid-90s fastballs all day that overpower the kids in the bus leagues, but a lack of command, control or consistency in his breaking stuff left him helpless against major-league bats. Oviedo has four pitches, a bulldog mentality and an ideal starter's frame but if the development staff can't sand away all those rough edges he's destined for middle relief.

YEAR	TEAM	LVL	AGE	WHIP	ERA	DRA-	WARP	MPH	FB%	WHF	CSP
2018	PEO	LO-A	20	1.54	4.22	92	1.3				
2019	PMB	HI-A	21	1.22	1.60	87	0.3				
2019	SPR	AA	21	1.63	5.65	130	-1.9				
2020	STL	MLB	22	1.38	5.47	134	-0.2	97.0	56.1%	21.5%	
2021 FS	STL	MLB	23	1.58	5.46	119	-0.2	97.0	56.1%	21.5%	47.2%
2021 DC	STL	MLB	23	1.58	5.46	119	-0.1	97.0	56.1%	21.5%	47.2%

Johan Oviedo, continued

Pitch Shape vs LHH

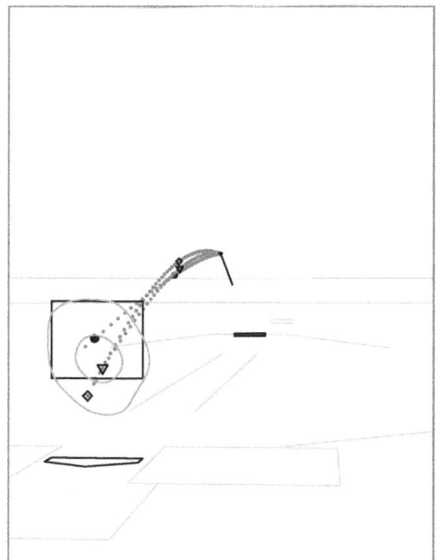

Pitch Shape vs RHH

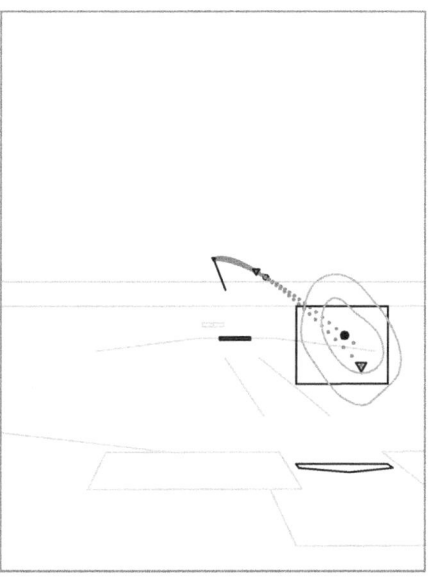

Type	Frequency	Velocity	H Movement	V Movement
● Fastball	56.1%	95.1 [108]	-3.2 [117]	-17.2 [94]
▲ Changeup	3.8%	87.6 [110]	-10.2 [108]	-23.2 [112]
▽ Slider	29.7%	85.1 [105]	5.7 [102]	-33.2 [101]
◇ Curveball	10.4%	77.3 [95]	10.3 [111]	-48.3 [100]

Daniel Ponce de Leon   RHP

Born: 01/16/92   Age: 29   Bats: R   Throws: R
Height: 6'3"   Weight: 200   Origin: Round 9, 2014 Draft (#285 overall)

YEAR	TEAM	LVL	AGE	W	L	SV	G	GS	IP	H	HR	BB/9	K/9	K	GB%	BABIP
2018	MEM	AAA	26	9	4	0	19	18	96^1	69	4	4.7	10.3	110	28.8%	.275
2018	STL	MLB	26	0	2	1	11	4	33	24	2	3.5	8.5	31	35.6%	.259
2019	MEM	AAA	27	8	4	0	16	16	84^1	62	7	4.6	9.2	86	35.9%	.256
2019	STL	MLB	27	1	2	0	13	8	48^2	36	6	4.8	9.6	52	45.5%	.256
2020	STL	MLB	28	1	3	0	9	8	32^2	23	8	5.5	12.4	45	28.9%	.221
2021 FS	STL	MLB	29	9	8	0	26	26	150	119	20	5.0	10.3	170	36.0%	.269
2021 DC	STL	MLB	29	5	5	0	22	16	81	64	10	5.0	10.3	92	36.0%	.269

Comparables: Carlos Martínez, Alec Mills, Chris Stratton

Last summer the world was awash in messages telling us to "avoid contact," and clearly Ponce de Leon took that to heart. Like his teammate Genesis Cabrera, less than half of the batters facing Ponce de Leon put the ball in play—not counting the big pile of dingers he allowed, a natural by-product of his league-leading fly-ball rate. His four-seamer sits in the low 90s with good rise and movement and can be an elite pitch when he commands it, especially high in the zone. But too often he misses his spot, leading to walks and gopher balls and crooked numbers on the scoreboard. Ponce de Leon has a decent hook and a cutter that took two steps forward last year, giving him a starter's arsenal that probably works best in relief.

YEAR	TEAM	LVL	AGE	WHIP	ERA	DRA-	WARP	MPH	FB%	WHF	CSP
2018	MEM	AAA	26	1.24	2.24	82	1.9				
2018	STL	MLB	26	1.12	2.73	78	0.6	95.5	61.8%	28.0%	
2019	MEM	AAA	27	1.25	2.88	50	3.4				
2019	STL	MLB	27	1.27	3.70	72	1.1	95.6	70.6%	27.0%	
2020	STL	MLB	28	1.32	4.96	110	0.1	95.2	61.1%	31.4%	
2021 FS	STL	MLB	29	1.35	3.97	92	2.1	95.4	65.1%	29.1%	45.1%
2021 DC	STL	MLB	29	1.35	3.97	92	1.0	95.4	65.1%	29.1%	45.1%

Daniel Ponce de Leon, continued

Pitch Shape vs LHH

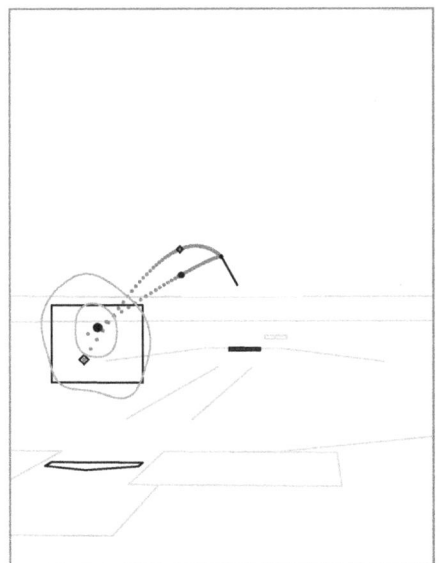

Pitch Shape vs RHH

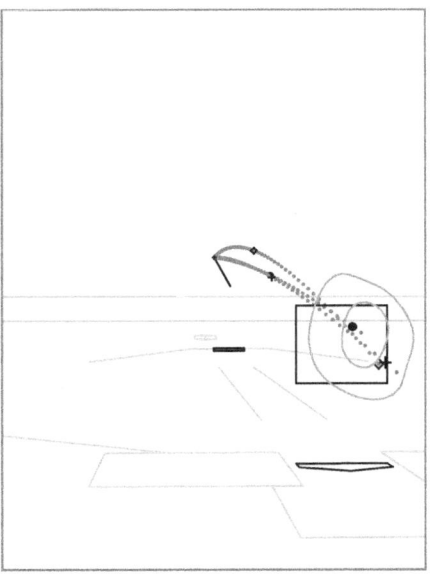

Type	Frequency	Velocity	H Movement	V Movement
● Fastball	61.1%	93.4 [103]	-8.4 [92]	-11.7 [110]
+ Cutter	13.3%	88.2 [99]	1.6 [98]	-25.4 [95]
▲ Changeup	3.9%	86.5 [105]	-13.9 [88]	-24.7 [108]
◇ Curveball	21.7%	77.9 [97]	7.2 [98]	-55.4 [84]

St. Louis Cardinals 2021

Alex Reyes RHP
Born: 08/29/94   Age: 26   Bats: R   Throws: R
Height: 6'4"   Weight: 220   Origin: International Free Agent, 2012

YEAR	TEAM	LVL	AGE	W	L	SV	G	GS	IP	H	HR	BB/9	K/9	K	GB%	BABIP
2018	SPR	AA	23	1	0	0	1	1	7²	1	0	3.5	15.3	13	20.0%	.111
2018	MEM	AAA	23	1	0	0	1	1	7	1	0	1.3	16.7	13	22.2%	.125
2018	STL	MLB	23	0	0	0	1	1	4	3	0	4.5	4.5	2	40.0%	.300
2019	PMB	HI-A	24	0	1	0	2	2	9¹	9	0	2.9	10.6	11	53.8%	.346
2019	MEM	AAA	24	1	3	0	10	7	28	27	5	7.7	12.2	38	37.7%	.355
2019	STL	MLB	24	0	1	0	4	0	3	2	1	18.0	3.0	1	30.0%	.111
2020	STL	MLB	25	2	1	1	15	1	19²	14	1	6.4	12.4	27	35.6%	.302
2021 FS	STL	MLB	26	2	2	7	57	0	50	39	6	6.0	11.7	64	38.1%	.288
2021 DC	STL	MLB	26	2	2	7	45	0	52.7	42	6	6.0	11.7	68	38.1%	.288

Comparables: Lucas Sims, Jake Faria, Antonio Senzatela

After all the struggles, it turned out to be as easy as one-two-three.

Game One. One former top prospect on the bump, one at the dish.

Two on. Two out. Two runs ahead. Two innings left in a playoff game. Tatis digs in. Reyes takes two deep breaths, rocks back and fires.

Three pitches. Three fastballs, all triple-digit. The third runs inside and Tatis fists it to short. Out number three. Then three more, and a postseason save. Three lost seasons, gone but not forgotten.

After years of injuries and setbacks—all of them unfortunate, some of them self-inflicted—it was both a joy and a relief to watch Reyes at long last earn his moment in the sun. The explosive fastball, hammer curve and diving slider, the strikeouts and the awkward swings, are all still there. So are the free passes and the questions about his role. Four years ago in this space we wrote that it's nearly impossible to thrive in a starting role while walking 12 percent of the batters you face; Reyes has now walked nearly 15 percent in his staccato big league career. His future should be in the late innings, but with Reyes it's almost never that easy.

YEAR	TEAM	LVL	AGE	WHIP	ERA	DRA-	WARP	MPH	FB%	WHF	CSP
2018	SPR	AA	23	0.52	0.00	10	0.5				
2018	MEM	AAA	23	0.29	0.00	17	0.4				
2018	STL	MLB	23	1.25	0.00	182	-0.1	96.9	57.5%	10.3%	
2019	PMB	HI-A	24	1.29	1.93	75	0.2				
2019	MEM	AAA	24	1.82	7.39	106	0.4				
2019	STL	MLB	24	2.67	15.00	136	0.0	98.8	59.4%	16.7%	
2020	STL	MLB	25	1.42	3.20	83	0.4	99.3	60.4%	34.6%	
2021 FS	*STL*	*MLB*	*26*	*1.47*	*4.26*	*96*	*0.3*	*99.1*	*60.2%*	*31.4%*	*42.9%*
2021 DC	*STL*	*MLB*	*26*	*1.47*	*4.26*	*96*	*0.4*	*99.1*	*60.2%*	*31.4%*	*42.9%*

St. Louis Cardinals 2021

Alex Reyes, continued

Pitch Shape vs LHH

Pitch Shape vs RHH

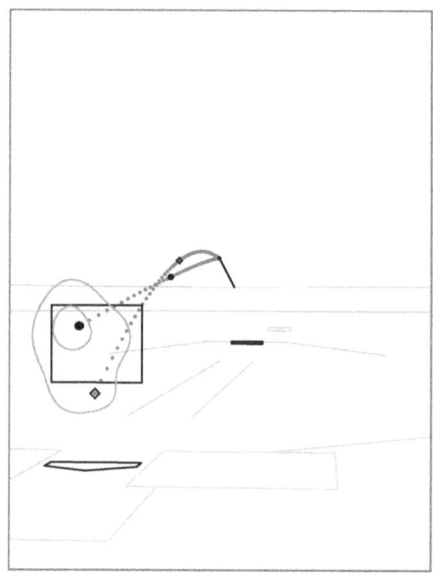
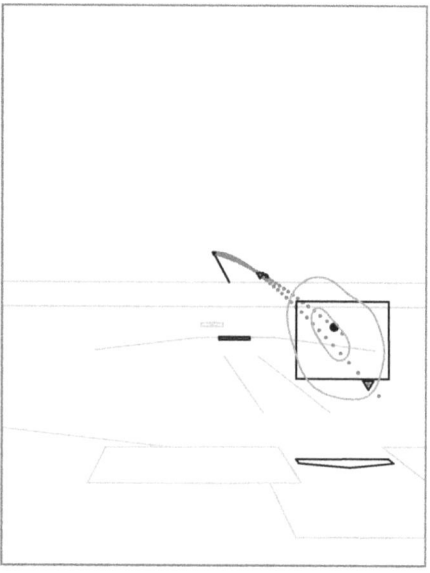

Type	Frequency	Velocity	H Movement	V Movement
● Fastball	49.1%	97.8 [116]	-5.6 [105]	-9.4 [116]
□ Sinker	10.7%	98 [129]	-11.6 [111]	-12.1 [127]
▲ Changeup	4.0%	90.9 [122]	-9.8 [110]	-20.5 [119]
▽ Slider	18.5%	87.1 [114]	5.9 [102]	-32.1 [105]
◇ Curveball	16.6%	82.1 [114]	7.4 [99]	-54.9 [86]

Adam Wainwright RHP

Born: 08/30/81   Age: 39   Bats: R   Throws: R
Height: 6'7"   Weight: 230   Origin: Round 1, 2000 Draft (#29 overall)

YEAR	TEAM	LVL	AGE	W	L	SV	G	GS	IP	H	HR	BB/9	K/9	K	GB%	BABIP
2018	SPR	AA	36	1	0	0	3	3	10	5	0	0.0	8.1	9	42.3%	.192
2018	MEM	AAA	36	1	0	0	2	2	9	8	0	4.0	11.0	11	38.1%	.381
2018	STL	MLB	36	2	4	0	8	8	40^1	41	5	4.0	8.9	40	47.9%	.319
2019	STL	MLB	37	14	10	0	31	31	171^2	181	22	3.4	8.0	153	48.1%	.323
2020	STL	MLB	38	5	3	0	10	10	65^2	54	9	2.1	7.4	54	42.9%	.247
2021 FS	STL	MLB	39	9	8	0	26	26	150	146	20	3.1	8.2	136	45.3%	.292
2021 DC	STL	MLB	39	8	7	0	24	24	128.7	125	17	3.1	8.2	116	45.3%	.292

Comparables: Jim Bunning, Gaylord Perry, Fergie Jenkins

It's been years since Wainwright led the league in anything but affability, yet last year Uncle Charlie was back in black ink after pacing the league in complete games. Sure, there were only two, and one was of the shortened COVID doubleheader variety, but the other was a bona fide 120-pitch gem on his 39th birthday. Wainwright remained both durable and productive last year, silently dissecting lineups while long-time bridge partner Yadier Molina sent out signals only the two of them understand. Waino and Yadi have started 289 games together, fourth on the all-time battery list and only 35 behind leaders Mickey Lolich and Bill Freehan. Health, money or roster decisions might get in the way, but they might just have enough gas left in the tank to get there.

YEAR	TEAM	LVL	AGE	WHIP	ERA	DRA-	WARP	MPH	FB%	WHF	CSP
2018	SPR	AA	36	0.50	0.00	92	0.1				
2018	MEM	AAA	36	1.33	0.00	64	0.3				
2018	STL	MLB	36	1.46	4.46	84	0.7	91.9	37.9%	23.7%	
2019	STL	MLB	37	1.43	4.19	93	2.2	91.9	38.4%	19.6%	
2020	STL	MLB	38	1.05	3.15	97	0.7	91.4	36.7%	24.2%	
2021 FS	STL	MLB	39	1.32	4.08	98	1.6	91.8	37.9%	21.3%	47.7%
2021 DC	STL	MLB	39	1.32	4.08	98	1.4	91.8	37.9%	21.3%	47.7%

St. Louis Cardinals 2021

Adam Wainwright, continued

Pitch Shape vs LHH

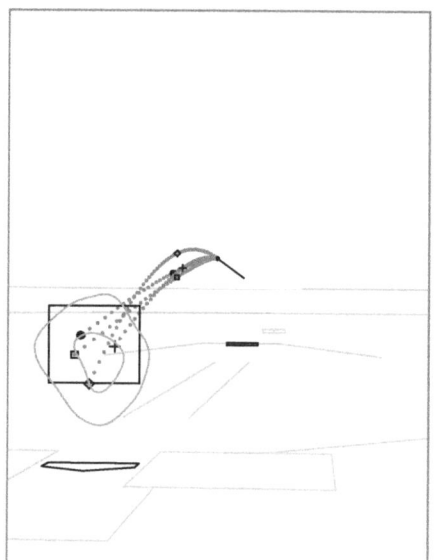

Pitch Shape vs RHH

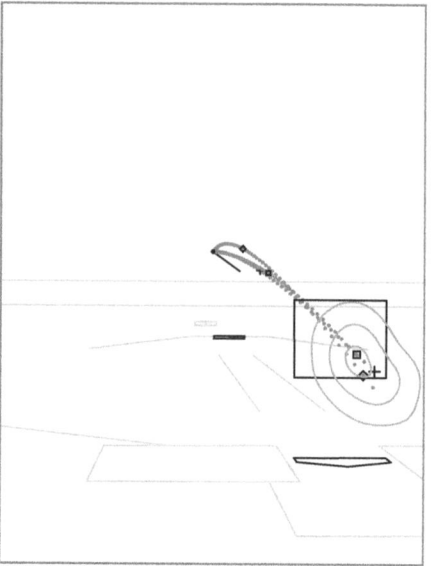

Type	Frequency	Velocity	H Movement	V Movement
● Fastball	9.7%	89.4 [90]	-2 [123]	-17.4 [94]
□ Sinker	27.0%	89.6 [85]	-10.9 [116]	-20.4 [100]
+ Cutter	22.6%	85.3 [81]	5.2 [122]	-27.9 [86]
◇ Curveball	38.3%	73.8 [81]	14.9 [130]	-58.8 [77]

Tyler Webb   LHP

Born: 07/20/90   Age: 30   Bats: L   Throws: L
Height: 6'5"   Weight: 240   Origin: Round 10, 2013 Draft (#314 overall)

YEAR	TEAM	LVL	AGE	W	L	SV	G	GS	IP	H	HR	BB/9	K/9	K	GB%	BABIP
2018	MEM	AAA	27	0	0	0	11	1	19.2	9	1	1.8	9.6	21	38.6%	.190
2018	ELP	AAA	27	1	1	0	19	0	22	20	1	3.3	11.5	28	37.5%	.345
2018	STL	MLB	27	0	0	0	18	0	15.1	16	1	3.5	6.5	11	29.2%	.326
2018	SD	MLB	27	0	1	0	4	0	5	6	2	5.4	7.2	4	41.2%	.267
2019	MEM	AAA	28	0	1	0	5	0	6.2	7	0	2.7	6.8	5	45.0%	.350
2019	STL	MLB	28	2	1	1	65	0	55	33	7	3.8	7.9	48	41.2%	.187
2020	STL	MLB	29	1	1	1	21	0	21.2	17	2	2.9	7.9	19	39.3%	.259
2021 FS	*STL*	*MLB*	*30*	*2*	*2*	*0*	*57*	*0*	*50*	*44*	*7*	*3.0*	*8.6*	*48*	*40.4%*	*.272*
2021 DC	*STL*	*MLB*	*30*	*2*	*2*	*0*	*50*	*0*	*52.7*	*46*	*7*	*3.0*	*8.6*	*50*	*40.4%*	*.272*

Comparables: Shawn Armstrong, Mike Morin, Nick Wittgren

The new "three-batter minimum" rule forced lefty specialist Webb to face more right-handed bats last year. A career-killer? Maybe not. He still put up his usual decent numbers, proving true the old adage "you can take the LOOGY out of the game, eventually, but you can't take the game out of the LOOGY."

YEAR	TEAM	LVL	AGE	WHIP	ERA	DRA-	WARP	MPH	FB%	WHF	CSP
2018	MEM	AAA	27	0.66	2.29	68	0.4				
2018	ELP	AAA	27	1.27	2.05	64	0.5				
2018	STL	MLB	27	1.43	1.76	150	-0.3	91.8	59.7%	22.9%	
2018	SD	MLB	27	1.80	12.60	184	-0.2	90.3	60.4%	23.7%	
2019	MEM	AAA	28	1.35	2.70	88	0.1				
2019	STL	MLB	28	1.02	3.76	81	0.8	91.5	65.3%	22.9%	
2020	STL	MLB	29	1.11	2.08	96	0.2	91.4	59.8%	25.3%	
2021 FS	*STL*	*MLB*	*30*	*1.22*	*3.61*	*89*	*0.6*	*91.5*	*62.9%*	*23.7%*	*49.9%*
2021 DC	*STL*	*MLB*	*30*	*1.22*	*3.61*	*89*	*0.6*	*91.5*	*62.9%*	*23.7%*	*49.9%*

Tyler Webb, continued

Pitch Shape vs LHH   **Pitch Shape vs RHH**

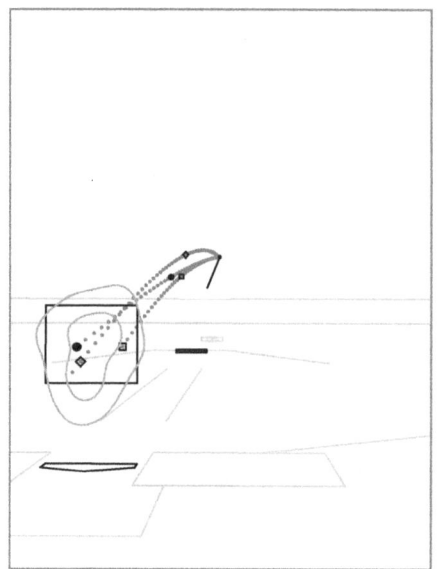 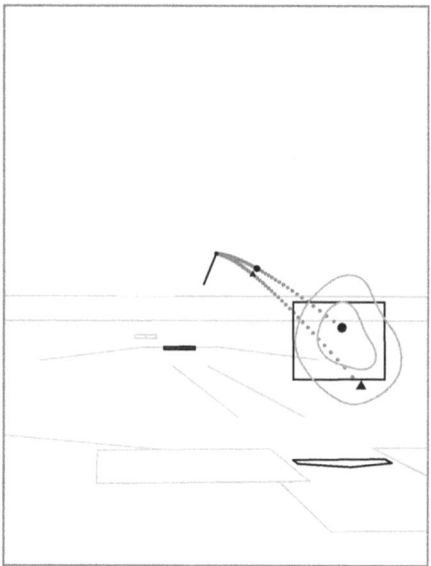

Type	Frequency	Velocity	H Movement	V Movement
● Fastball	40.8%	90.3 [93]	1.8 [124]	-14.8 [101]
☐ Sinker	19.1%	90.4 [89]	9.1 [129]	-15.9 [115]
▲ Changeup	23.7%	78.8 [75]	4.8 [137]	-24.7 [108]
◇ Curveball	16.5%	75 [86]	-4.2 [86]	-49 [99]

Jake Woodford   RHP

Born: 10/28/96   Age: 24   Bats: R   Throws: R
Height: 6'4"   Weight: 215   Origin: Round 1, 2015 Draft (#39 overall)

YEAR	TEAM	LVL	AGE	W	L	SV	G	GS	IP	H	HR	BB/9	K/9	K	GB%	BABIP
2018	SPR	AA	21	3	8	0	16	16	81	94	13	3.9	6.2	56	46.9%	.313
2018	MEM	AAA	21	5	5	0	12	12	64	64	5	3.8	6.3	45	36.2%	.295
2019	MEM	AAA	22	9	8	0	26	26	151^2	124	22	4.5	7.8	131	37.0%	.249
2020	STL	MLB	23	1	0	0	12	1	21	20	7	2.1	6.9	16	45.3%	.228
2021 FS	STL	MLB	24	2	3	0	57	0	50	51	8	4.6	7.3	40	39.8%	.291
2021 DC	STL	MLB	24	4	3	0	37	4	49	50	7	4.6	7.3	40	39.8%	.291

Comparables: Jonathan Hernández, Brad Hand, Enyel De Los Santos

Woodford may someday make it as a swingman but big-league hitters took him to the woodshed during his big league debut, homering once every three innings and posting slash stats reminiscent of a good Eddie Rosario season; it's not easy to register both a FIP nearing 7 and a WHIP nearing 1.

YEAR	TEAM	LVL	AGE	WHIP	ERA	DRA-	WARP	MPH	FB%	WHF	CSP
2018	SPR	AA	21	1.59	5.22	96	0.5				
2018	MEM	AAA	21	1.42	4.50	108	0.4				
2019	MEM	AAA	22	1.31	4.15	69	4.9				
2020	STL	MLB	23	1.19	5.57	113	0.0	94.3	77.8%	20.4%	
2021 FS	STL	MLB	24	1.55	5.32	119	-0.3	94.3	77.8%	20.4%	48.8%
2021 DC	STL	MLB	24	1.55	5.32	119	-0.2	94.3	77.8%	20.4%	48.8%

St. Louis Cardinals 2021

Jake Woodford, continued

Pitch Shape vs LHH

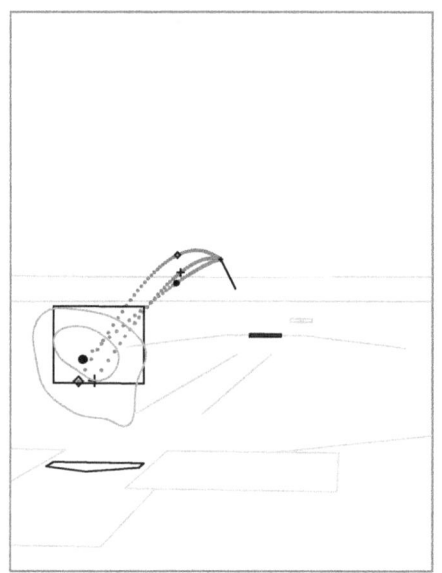

Pitch Shape vs RHH

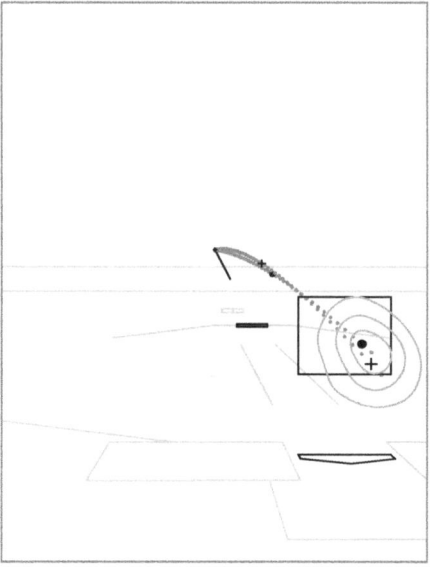

Type	Frequency	Velocity	H Movement	V Movement
● Fastball	49.7%	93.1 [102]	-5.4 [106]	-15.9 [98]
+ Cutter	26.9%	84.8 [77]	3.3 [109]	-35.3 [57]
◇ Curveball	21.1%	76.5 [92]	9.3 [107]	-58.5 [77]

PLAYER COMMENTS WITHOUT GRAPHS

Austin Dean LF
Born: 10/14/93   Age: 27   Bats: R   Throws: R
Height: 6'0"   Weight: 215   Origin: Round 4, 2012 Draft (#137 overall)

YEAR	TEAM	LVL	AGE	PA	R	2B	3B	HR	RBI	BB	K	SB	CS	AVG/OBP/SLG
2018	JAX	AA	24	88	13	8	1	3	14	6	7	0	0	.420/.466/.654
2018	NO	AAA	24	358	58	12	4	9	54	33	49	2	2	.326/.397/.475
2018	MIA	MLB	24	122	16	4	0	4	14	7	22	1	0	.221/.279/.363
2019	NO	AAA	25	282	48	19	1	18	57	28	52	4	3	.337/.401/.635
2019	MIA	MLB	25	189	17	14	0	6	21	9	47	0	2	.225/.261/.404
2020	STL	MLB	26	7	1	1	0	0	0	3	2	0	0	.250/.571/.500
2021 FS	STL	MLB	27	600	71	27	2	21	76	45	143	0	1	.248/.307/.427
2021 DC	STL	MLB	27	229	27	10	1	8	29	17	54	0	0	.248/.307/.427

Comparables: Henry Rodriguez, Mark Smith, Craig Monroe

Dean has spent the last few years alternately raking in the high minors and face-planting in the National League, and, at age 27, fits one of the game's most unfortunate labels: Quad-A tweener.

YEAR	TEAM	LVL	AGE	PA	DRC+	BABIP	BRR	FRAA	WARP
2018	JAX	AA	24	88	196	.437	-2.0	LF(21): 0.5	0.8
2018	NO	AAA	24	358	134	.360	0.5	LF(45): -2.2, RF(37): -0.8	1.5
2018	MIA	MLB	24	122	92	.241	1.1	LF(31): 0.5	0.4
2019	NO	AAA	25	282	147	.364	2.2	1B(26): 0.7, LF(22): 2.0, RF(11): 1.3	2.6
2019	MIA	MLB	25	189	77	.270	1.0	LF(44): -2.8, 1B(5): -0.1, RF(5): 0.3	-0.2
2020	STL	MLB	26	7	85	.500		LF(2): 0.0, 1B(1): -0.0, RF(1): -0.0	0.0
2021 FS	STL	MLB	27	600	103	.294	-0.6	RF 0, LF 1	1.7
2021 DC	STL	MLB	27	229	103	.294	-0.2	RF 0, LF 0	0.6

Nolan Gorman 3B
Born: 05/10/00   Age: 21   Bats: L   Throws: R
Height: 6'1"   Weight: 210   Origin: Round 1, 2018 Draft (#19 overall)

YEAR	TEAM	LVL	AGE	PA	R	2B	3B	HR	RBI	BB	K	SB	CS	AVG/OBP/SLG
2018	JC	ROK	18	167	41	10	1	11	28	24	37	1	3	.350/.443/.664
2018	PEO	LO-A	18	107	8	3	0	6	16	10	39	0	2	.202/.280/.426
2019	PEO	LO-A	19	282	41	14	3	10	41	32	79	2	0	.241/.344/.448
2019	PMB	HI-A	19	230	24	16	3	5	21	13	73	0	1	.256/.304/.428
2021 FS	STL	MLB	21	600	51	22	3	13	57	43	224	0	1	.192/.258/.321

Comparables: Ryan McMahon, Austin Riley, Tyler Goeddel

St. Louis Cardinals 2021

Last year in this space, after noting that Gorman would predictably start at one minor-league level, dominate, gain a promotion and then see both his strikeouts and power spike, we asked the universe to "get more creative writers." If that plea in any way caused the universe to shake things up by inviting, y'know, 2020 upon us, please accept our apologies. Gorman spent last summer at the club's alternate training site working to reduce his worrisome strikeout rate while retaining his light-tower power—a story archetype writers call "Overcoming the Monster." Here's hoping the next chapter is revealed later this year.

YEAR	TEAM	LVL	AGE	PA	DRC+	BABIP	BRR	FRAA	WARP
2018	JC	ROK	18	167		.411			
2018	PEO	LO-A	18	107	77	.255	-0.5	3B(25): 3.9	0.3
2019	PEO	LO-A	19	282	128	.312	0.4	3B(51): 8.4	2.6
2019	PMB	HI-A	19	230	107	.365	-2.1	3B(49): -5.9	0.0
2021 FS	STL	MLB	21	600	57	.295	-0.5	3B 1	-2.1

Ivan Herrera C
Born: 06/01/00   Age: 21   Bats: R   Throws: R
Height: 5'11"   Weight: 220   Origin: International Free Agent, 2016

YEAR	TEAM	LVL	AGE	PA	R	2B	3B	HR	RBI	BB	K	SB	CS	AVG/OBP/SLG
2018	CAR	ROK	18	130	23	6	4	1	25	11	20	1	1	.348/.423/.500
2019	PEO	LO-A	19	291	41	10	0	8	42	35	56	1	1	.286/.381/.423
2019	PMB	HI-A	19	65	7	0	0	1	5	5	16	0	0	.276/.338/.328
2021 FS	STL	MLB	21	600	63	21	2	11	58	34	178	1	1	.224/.278/.333
2021 DC	STL	MLB	21	34	3	1	0	0	3	1	10	0	0	.224/.278/.333

Comparables: Chance Sisco, Wil Myers, Hank Conger

Herrera vaulted up prospect lists after a standout 2019 season where he showcased a well-rounded set of tools and a surprisingly mature approach for a teenager in full-season leagues. The young Panamanian continued to impress during spring training, where he was an eager participant in Yadi's kaffeeklatsch, and at the team's summer complex, where he worked hard to implement the master's lessons on defense and leadership. Herrera has the tools and the makeup to grow into a solid receiver, a swing that can generate average power and a birth certificate indicating he could be the first St. Louis catching prospect in a generation to be ready for the big-league job at the precise moment the big-league job is ready for him.

YEAR	TEAM	LVL	AGE	PA	DRC+	BABIP	BRR	FRAA	WARP
2018	CAR	ROK	18	130		.409			
2019	PEO	LO-A	19	291	138	.337	-0.1	C(64): -1.0	2.4
2019	PMB	HI-A	19	65	116	.357	-1.1	C(18): -0.1	0.3
2021 FS	STL	MLB	21	600	71	.306	-0.6	C -1	0.1
2021 DC	STL	MLB	21	34	71	.306	0.0	C 0	0.0

Andrew Knizner C

Born: 02/03/95 Age: 26 Bats: R Throws: R
Height: 6'1" Weight: 225 Origin: Round 7, 2016 Draft (#226 overall)

YEAR	TEAM	LVL	AGE	PA	R	2B	3B	HR	RBI	BB	K	SB	CS	AVG/OBP/SLG
2018	SPR	AA	23	313	39	13	0	7	41	23	40	0	1	.313/.365/.434
2018	MEM	AAA	23	61	3	5	0	0	4	4	8	0	0	.315/.383/.407
2019	MEM	AAA	24	280	41	10	0	12	34	24	37	2	0	.276/.357/.463
2019	STL	MLB	24	58	7	2	0	2	7	4	14	2	0	.226/.293/.377
2020	STL	MLB	25	17	1	1	0	0	4	0	5	0	0	.250/.235/.312
2021 FS	STL	MLB	26	600	66	25	1	17	70	39	124	0	1	.248/.310/.396
2021 DC	STL	MLB	26	128	14	5	0	3	15	8	26	0	0	.248/.310/.396

Comparables: Hank Conger, Elias Díaz, Curtis Thigpen

YEAR	TEAM	P. COUNT	FRM RUNS	BLK RUNS	THRW RUNS	TOT RUNS
2019	STL	2098	-4.0	-0.4	0.1	-4.3
2020	STL	679	-0.3	0.0	0.0	-0.3
2021	STL	15632	-15.4	2.5	0.8	-12.2
2021	STL	15632	-15.4	0.4	0.8	-14.2

André-François Raffray, age 47, once signed a contract that required him to pay Jeanne Calment, age 90, a generous monthly stipend until she died, after which Raffray would inherit her apartment. For 30 years the French lawyer waited and watched as Calment continued to dance, cycle, smoke and cash his checks until Raffray passed away, his patience unfulfilled. You know where we're going with this. Knizner has been the latest Raffray to haunt the Cardinals clubhouse, fated to spend his mid-20s watching Yadier Molina stare down Father Time. He's a bat-first backstop with a career .303/.369/.461 minor league line and a compact swing that can make enough noise to drown out his often sketchy receiving skills. Knizner has struggled mightily at the plate during his first few trips to The Lou, however, and if he doesn't figure out big league pitching soon he won't be around long enough to inherit anyone's starting gig behind the dish.

YEAR	TEAM	LVL	AGE	PA	DRC+	BABIP	BRR	FRAA	WARP
2018	SPR	AA	23	313	133	.339	-1.4	C(74): -7.3	1.0
2018	MEM	AAA	23	61	116	.370	-0.1	C(16): 1.8	0.5
2019	MEM	AAA	24	280	111	.281	-0.8	C(61): -17.2	0.2
2019	STL	MLB	24	58	82	.270	0.5	C(16): -4.4, 1B(1): -0.0	-0.2
2020	STL	MLB	25	17	71	.333		C(7): -0.1	-0.1
2021 FS	STL	MLB	26	600	98	.289	-0.9	C -50, 1B 0	-3.0
2021 DC	STL	MLB	26	128	98	.289	-0.2	C -14	-1.0

Brad Miller 2B

Born: 10/18/89 Age: 31 Bats: L Throws: R
Height: 6'2" Weight: 195 Origin: Round 2, 2011 Draft (#62 overall)

YEAR	TEAM	LVL	AGE	PA	R	2B	3B	HR	RBI	BB	K	SB	CS	AVG/OBP/SLG
2018	RMV	AAA	28	31	4	0	0	1	2	3	9	1	0	.185/.258/.296
2018	TB	MLB	28	174	16	10	1	5	21	16	51	0	0	.256/.322/.429
2018	MIL	MLB	28	80	5	3	1	2	8	6	31	0	0	.230/.287/.378
2019	SWB	AAA	29	163	31	9	1	10	29	24	40	1	3	.294/.399/.596
2019	CLE	MLB	29	40	4	3	0	1	4	4	10	1	0	.250/.325/.417
2019	PHI	MLB	29	130	22	3	1	12	21	11	35	1	0	.263/.331/.610
2020	STL	MLB	30	171	21	8	1	7	25	25	46	1	0	.232/.357/.451
2021 FS	STL	MLB	31	600	73	25	3	25	80	70	172	5	3	.230/.326/.439
2021 DC	STL	MLB	31	239	29	10	1	10	31	27	68	2	1	.230/.326/.439

Comparables: Woodie Held, Stephen Drew, Jose Valentin

The fact that Miller, a man who over the previous season-and-a-half had been traded by the Rays and released or sold by the Brewers, Dodgers, Cleveland, Yankees and Phillies, wound up co-leading St. Louis with seven home runs last year speaks well of his resilience and poorly of the Cardinals offense. The vagabond lefty came out hot, slashing .317/.450/.619 through September 1, before struggling mightily the rest of the way. It's that streakiness, alongside his inability to play in the middle of the diamond, which has left Miller riding the rails so frequently despite his obvious offensive talent. At least he can now say he's the greatest DH in Cardinals history, which ought to count for something in this crazy mixed-up world.

YEAR	TEAM	LVL	AGE	PA	DRC+	BABIP	BRR	FRAA	WARP
2018	RMV	AAA	28	31	46	.222	-0.7	SS(6): 0.2, 2B(1): 0.1	-0.1
2018	TB	MLB	28	174	81	.343	-0.6	1B(35): -2.1, 2B(6): 0.2	-0.4
2018	MIL	MLB	28	80	83	.366	-0.7	2B(15): 0.1, SS(6): -0.4, 1B(1): 0.0	0.0
2019	SWB	AAA	29	163	132	.341	-0.7	2B(13): -0.9, LF(11): 0.6, 3B(10): -1.3	0.8
2019	CLE	MLB	29	40	81	.320	0.7	2B(13): 0.4	0.1
2019	PHI	MLB	29	130	128	.268	0.3	3B(19): 0.4, LF(16): 1.3, SS(1): 0.0	1.1
2020	STL	MLB	30	171	104	.289	-0.5	3B(15): -0.0, SS(2): -0.1, 2B(1): 0.1	0.3
2021 FS	STL	MLB	31	600	107	.292	0.0	1B -1, 2B 0	1.9
2021 DC	STL	MLB	31	239	107	.292	0.0	1B 0, 2B 0	0.7

John Nogowski 1B

Born: 01/05/93 Age: 28 Bats: R Throws: L
Height: 6'0" Weight: 245 Origin: Round 34, 2014 Draft (#1032 overall)

YEAR	TEAM	LVL	AGE	PA	R	2B	3B	HR	RBI	BB	K	SB	CS	AVG/OBP/SLG
2018	CAR	ROK	25	34	5	0	0	0	3	3	4	1	0	.345/.412/.345
2018	SPR	AA	25	347	41	10	0	12	61	41	21	0	2	.309/.392/.463
2019	MEM	AAA	26	463	77	22	1	15	75	69	54	1	2	.295/.413/.476
2020	STL	MLB	27	4	0	0	0	0	0	0	1	0	0	.250/.250/.250
2021 FS	STL	MLB	28	600	75	28	1	15	70	60	102	0	1	.264/.345/.412
2021 DC	STL	MLB	28	180	22	8	0	4	21	18	30	0	0	.264/.345/.412

Comparables: Daric Barton, David Cooper, Dan Johnson

A former 34th-round pick, Nogowski made it all the way to the Show last summer. He's walked more than he's whiffed in his minor-league career, but his lack of a first baseman's power makes him more of a no-go-ski going forward.

YEAR	TEAM	LVL	AGE	PA	DRC+	BABIP	BRR	FRAA	WARP
2018	CAR	ROK	25	34		.385			
2018	SPR	AA	25	347	148	.296	-2.0	1B(78): 15.0, LF(2): -0.1	2.7
2019	MEM	AAA	26	463	128	.308	-6.2	1B(107): 12.1, P(3): -0.1	2.8
2020	STL	MLB	27	4	66	.333	-0.4	1B(1): 0.0	-0.1
2021 FS	STL	MLB	28	600	115	.297	-1.0	1B 3, LF 0	2.2
2021 DC	STL	MLB	28	180	115	.297	-0.3	1B 1	0.7

Ali Sánchez C

Born: 01/20/97 Age: 24 Bats: R Throws: R
Height: 6'1" Weight: 200 Origin: International Free Agent, 2013

YEAR	TEAM	LVL	AGE	PA	R	2B	3B	HR	RBI	BB	K	SB	CS	AVG/OBP/SLG
2018	COL	LO-A	21	205	26	11	1	4	22	10	23	1	1	.259/.293/.389
2018	STL	HI-A	21	142	11	9	0	2	16	5	15	1	1	.274/.296/.385
2019	BNG	AA	22	294	28	13	0	1	30	23	52	1	0	.278/.337/.337
2019	SYR	AAA	22	65	5	4	0	0	3	5	11	0	1	.179/.277/.250
2020	NYM	MLB	23	10	0	0	0	0	0	1	3	0	0	.111/.200/.111
2021 FS	STL	MLB	24	600	64	25	1	9	58	37	135	1	1	.221/.273/.322
2021 DC	STL	MLB	24	30	3	1	0	0	2	1	6	0	0	.221/.273/.322

Comparables: Austin Romine, Gary Sánchez, Meibrys Viloria

Sanchez made his debut in 2020, but is far more likely to be a Triple-A mainstay than to see any extended action in the big leagues. HIs defense may be rock-solid, but his bat is mostly vapor.

YEAR	TEAM	P. COUNT	FRM RUNS	BLK RUNS	THRW RUNS	TOT RUNS
2019	SYR	2336	0.9	0.0	0.3	1.1
2019	BNG	9109	-1.7	0.0	2.0	0.3
2020	NYM	539	0.0	0.0	0.0	0.0
2021	STL	2405	-0.1	-0.1	-0.1	-0.3
2021	STL	2405	-0.1	-0.3	-0.1	-0.5

St. Louis Cardinals 2021

YEAR	TEAM	LVL	AGE	PA	DRC+	BABIP	BRR	FRAA	WARP
2018	COL	LO-A	21	205	118	.274	0.4	C(36): 1.4	1.0
2018	STL	HI-A	21	142	98	.292	-0.9	C(27): -0.1	0.1
2019	BNG	AA	22	294	116	.341	-1.9	C(65): 1.2	1.7
2019	SYR	AAA	22	65	57	.217	-0.5	C(20): 1.2	0.1
2020	NYM	MLB	23	10	84	.167	0.2	C(5): -0.1	0.1
2021 FS	STL	MLB	24	600	66	.273	-0.9	C -5	-0.7
2021 DC	STL	MLB	24	30	66	.273	0.0	C 0	0.0

Edmundo Sosa SS
Born: 03/06/96 Age: 25 Bats: R Throws: R
Height: 6'0" Weight: 210 Origin: International Free Agent, 2012

YEAR	TEAM	LVL	AGE	PA	R	2B	3B	HR	RBI	BB	K	SB	CS	AVG/OBP/SLG
2018	SPR	AA	22	279	34	17	1	7	32	9	52	1	2	.276/.308/.429
2018	MEM	AAA	22	209	31	13	0	5	27	13	42	5	2	.262/.321/.408
2018	STL	MLB	22	3	1	0	0	0	0	1	1	0	0	.000/.333/.000
2019	MEM	AAA	23	496	70	18	5	17	62	17	96	2	3	.291/.335/.466
2019	STL	MLB	23	10	2	0	0	0	0	1	2	1	0	.250/.400/.250
2021 FS	STL	MLB	25	600	60	25	2	15	68	26	154	1	1	.239/.282/.377
2021 DC	STL	MLB	25	222	22	9	0	5	25	9	56	0	0	.239/.282/.377

Comparables: Reid Brignac, Brent Lillibridge, Thairo Estrada

This is the point in the Cardinals chapter where we generally anoint our pick for the next second-tier prospect to take a big swig of Devil Magic brand hard seltzer; we're never right, of course, but…just watch hacktastic, vacuum-gloved middle infielder Sosa duplicate his uncharacteristically solid Memphis numbers at the keystone in Busch next year.

YEAR	TEAM	LVL	AGE	PA	DRC+	BABIP	BRR	FRAA	WARP
2018	SPR	AA	22	279	92	.319	1.4	SS(43): -4.8, 3B(11): 1.6, 2B(10): -2.0	-0.2
2018	MEM	AAA	22	209	88	.310	0.7	SS(28): 1.1, 2B(12): -0.3, 3B(10): -0.3	0.4
2018	STL	MLB	22	3	83	.000		2B(1): 0.0	0.0
2019	MEM	AAA	23	496	94	.332	0.7	SS(84): 4.0, 2B(17): 0.9, 3B(15): -1.3	2.2
2019	STL	MLB	23	10	84	.333	-0.1	2B(4): -0.1	0.0
2021 FS	STL	MLB	25	600	82	.299	-0.6	2B -1, SS 0	0.2
2021 DC	STL	MLB	25	222	82	.299	-0.2	2B 0, SS 0	0.1

Lane Thomas CF

Born: 08/23/95 Age: 25 Bats: R Throws: R
Height: 6'0" Weight: 185 Origin: Round 5, 2014 Draft (#144 overall)

YEAR	TEAM	LVL	AGE	PA	R	2B	3B	HR	RBI	BB	K	SB	CS	AVG/OBP/SLG
2018	SPR	AA	22	435	63	16	4	21	67	43	101	13	9	.260/.337/.487
2018	MEM	AAA	22	140	21	7	2	6	21	7	33	4	1	.275/.321/.496
2019	MEM	AAA	23	304	42	17	2	10	44	32	80	11	6	.268/.352/.460
2019	STL	MLB	23	44	6	0	1	4	12	4	8	1	1	.316/.409/.684
2020	STL	MLB	24	40	5	2	0	1	2	4	13	0	0	.111/.200/.250
2021 FS	STL	MLB	25	600	69	23	3	20	70	48	195	9	5	.221/.288/.393
2021 DC	STL	MLB	25	214	24	8	1	7	25	17	69	3	2	.221/.288/.393

Comparables: Brian Anderson, Harrison Bader, Jai Miller

The Cardinals have yet to really find out what they have in "Fast Lane" Thomas. He flashes a tantalizing speed-defense-power combo that can surely make you lose your mind but he hasn't stayed between the lines long enough to prove it's not a mirage, losing time to a broken wrist in 2019 and COVID-19 last summer. Thomas can dazzle in center field and is a blur on the basepaths, though he has yet to swipe bases with a high success rate. His bat is a work in progress with power that might only be fringe average, but he has a good approach, takes his walks and makes enough contact to keep his head above water. A healthy Thomas should make a fine fourth outfielder, and has an outside chance of growing into something more.

YEAR	TEAM	LVL	AGE	PA	DRC+	BABIP	BRR	FRAA	WARP
2018	SPR	AA	22	435	107	.298	-0.5	CF(83): 4.0, RF(10): -0.5	1.0
2018	MEM	AAA	22	140	100	.326	1.0	CF(32): 1.5	0.6
2019	MEM	AAA	23	304	97	.343	0.6	CF(37): 5.0, LF(32): -2.4, RF(3): -0.2	1.1
2019	STL	MLB	23	44	110	.308	0.3	CF(19): 2.1, RF(5): 0.4, LF(2): -0.1	0.5
2020	STL	MLB	24	40	79	.136	-0.1	RF(14): -0.0, CF(7): -0.3	-0.1
2021 FS	STL	MLB	25	600	89	.298	0.6	RF 1, CF 1	1.0
2021 DC	STL	MLB	25	214	89	.298	0.2	RF 0, CF 0	0.2

Jhon Torres RF

Born: 03/29/00 Age: 21 Bats: R Throws: R
Height: 6'4" Weight: 199 Origin: International Free Agent, 2016

YEAR	TEAM	LVL	AGE	PA	R	2B	3B	HR	RBI	BB	K	SB	CS	AVG/OBP/SLG
2018	INDB	ROK	18	111	16	3	0	4	16	11	24	3	0	.273/.351/.424
2018	CAR	ROK	18	75	11	6	0	4	14	8	13	1	1	.397/.493/.683
2019	JC	ROK+	19	133	24	9	0	6	17	19	36	0	2	.286/.391/.527
2019	PEO	LO-A	19	75	4	3	0	0	8	7	29	0	1	.167/.240/.212
2021 FS	STL	MLB	21	600	45	21	2	8	47	42	215	3	3	.188/.253/.278

Comparables: Teoscar Hernández, José Martínez, Gabriel Guerrero

Torres has the build, arm and raw power of a prototypical right fielder, and he has enough of an idea at the plate to turn his tools into consistent production. He's yet to conquer full-season ball, let alone the high minors, but there's plenty to like here.

YEAR	TEAM	LVL	AGE	PA	DRC+	BABIP	BRR	FRAA	WARP
2018	INDB	ROK	18	111		.324			
2018	CAR	ROK	18	75		.457			
2019	JC	ROK+	19	133		.366			
2019	PEO	LO-A	19	75	49	.282	-0.6	RF(20): 3.8	0.1
2021 FS	STL	MLB	21	600	47	.291	-0.3	RF 20, CF 0	-0.8

Jordan Walker 3B
Born: 05/22/02 Age: 19 Bats: R Throws: R
Height: 6'5" Weight: 220 Origin: Round 1, 2020 Draft (#21 overall)

The Cardinals' top pick last summer, Walker is a high ceiling prospect straight out of Central Casting. You want physicality? Tall and strong with an ideal frame that presages top shelf power. Athleticism? Soft hands and smooth movements that make him a good bet to stay in the infield. Intelligence and makeup? A Duke scholarship and parents who went to Harvard and MIT. Personal tie to St. Louis? Walker's mom got her Master's at Wash U. Myth-making, if apocryphal, story? Kid broke his grandmother's windshield hitting a home run in tee-ball. The road from draftee to star is long and arduous and nothing is guaranteed, but this is the clay from which legends can be sculpted.

Matt Wieters C

Born: 05/21/86   Age: 35   Bats: S   Throws: R
Height: 6'5"   Weight: 235   Origin: Round 1, 2007 Draft (#5 overall)

YEAR	TEAM	LVL	AGE	PA	R	2B	3B	HR	RBI	BB	K	SB	CS	AVG/OBP/SLG
2018	WAS	MLB	32	271	24	8	0	8	30	30	45	0	1	.238/.330/.374
2019	STL	MLB	33	183	15	4	0	11	27	12	47	1	1	.214/.268/.435
2020	STL	MLB	34	41	3	1	0	0	4	3	10	0	0	.200/.300/.229
2021 FS	*STL*	*MLB*	*35*	*600*	*59*	*20*	*1*	*18*	*65*	*49*	*147*	*2*	*1*	*.216/.286/.358*

Comparables: Erik Kratz, Miguel Montero, Jason Varitek

YEAR	TEAM	P. COUNT	FRM RUNS	BLK RUNS	THRW RUNS	TOT RUNS
2018	WAS	9180	-3.7	1.1	0.3	-2.2
2019	STL	6279	-8.7	1.2	0.3	-7.2
2020	STL	1742	-0.8	0.0	0.0	-0.8
2021	*STL*	*16650*	*-14.0*	*1.6*	*-0.8*	*-13.3*
2021	*STL*	*16650*	*-14.0*	*2.6*	*-0.8*	*-12.2*

Wieters remains a perfectly acceptable backup receiver and a long-term MLB survivor of the sort we would celebrate if he weren't Matt Wieters. The unfairness of that is understood by every bright middle schooler who received conflicting "A" and "Needs Improvement" marks for the same class. (Full disclosure: that describes many of us here at Baseball Prospectus). Wieters has overcome injuries, inconsistency and outlandish expectations to earn four All-Star nods and two Gold Gloves. He's among the top-50 catchers in career home runs, the top 100 in WARP and in Jay Jaffe's JAWS metric. Over his 12 seasons he's only signed one multi-year deal: a two-year pact with the Nats who still owe him for half of the deferred second year. Unlike so many players who the popular imagination labels as disappointments, Wieters isn't still playing because teams owe him money, but because teams still want to pay him money. Good on you, mate.

YEAR	TEAM	LVL	AGE	PA	DRC+	BABIP	BRR	FRAA	WARP
2018	WAS	MLB	32	271	100	.261	-0.8	C(73): -4.0	0.9
2019	STL	MLB	33	183	96	.223	-0.8	C(54): -7.4	0.0
2020	STL	MLB	34	41	78	.280	0.0	C(18): -0.1	-0.1
2021 FS	*STL*	*MLB*	*35*	*600*	*80*	*.260*	*-0.8*	*C -13*	*-0.5*

St. Louis Cardinals 2021

Justin Williams LF

Born: 08/20/95 Age: 25 Bats: L Throws: R
Height: 6'1" Weight: 235 Origin: Round 2, 2013 Draft (#52 overall)

YEAR	TEAM	LVL	AGE	PA	R	2B	3B	HR	RBI	BB	K	SB	CS	AVG/OBP/SLG
2018	DUR	AAA	22	386	41	18	0	8	46	25	81	4	3	.258/.312/.376
2018	MEM	AAA	22	76	8	3	0	3	11	5	17	0	1	.217/.276/.391
2018	TB	MLB	22	1	0	0	0	0	0	0	0	0	0	.000/.000/.000
2019	SPR	AA	23	61	7	1	0	1	3	4	17	1	0	.193/.246/.263
2019	MEM	AAA	23	119	20	5	0	7	26	16	30	0	0	.353/.437/.608
2020	STL	MLB	24	6	0	0	0	0	0	1	2	0	0	.200/.333/.200
2021 FS	STL	MLB	25	600	63	23	1	17	66	40	158	0	1	.230/.286/.374
2021 DC	STL	MLB	25	94	9	3	0	2	10	6	24	0	0	.230/.286/.374

Comparables: Fernando Martinez, Brandon Moss, Josh Kroeger

Williams, a slow-burn outfield prospect, has a solid corner-outfield glove and hits the ball hard but has yet to take consistent advantage of his tools. Last year we damned him with the faint praise of not being quite as good as Randy Arozarena; the Cardinals would be thrilled if that were true this year.

YEAR	TEAM	LVL	AGE	PA	DRC+	BABIP	BRR	FRAA	WARP
2018	DUR	AAA	22	386	97	.315	-2.7	RF(80): 13.7, LF(2): 1.0	1.3
2018	MEM	AAA	22	76	85	.240	-1.1	LF(10): 4.2, RF(7): 0.9	0.4
2018	TB	MLB	22	1	82	.000		RF(1): -0.0	0.0
2019	SPR	AA	23	61	56	.256	-0.1	LF(12): -0.7, RF(2): -0.1	-0.2
2019	MEM	AAA	23	119	145	.439	-0.5	RF(25): 3.9	1.2
2020	STL	MLB	24	6	71	.333		RF(2): -0.1	0.0
2021 FS	STL	MLB	25	600	80	.290	-0.8	RF 7, LF 2	0.5
2021 DC	STL	MLB	25	94	80	.290	-0.1	RF 1, LF 0	0.1

Masyn Winn SS

Born: 03/21/02 Age: 19 Bats: R Throws: R
Height: 5'11" Weight: 180 Origin: Round 2, 2020 Draft (#54 overall)

A second-round pick, Winn is a high-energy two-way player with speed, power potential, soft hands and athleticism at shortstop, as well as high-90s velocity on the mound. There's lots of work to do, but the Cardinals have started developing him as both a pitcher and a position player, hoping for a win-win.

Junior Fernández   RHP
Born: 03/02/97   Age: 24   Bats: R   Throws: R
Height: 6'3"   Weight: 215   Origin: International Free Agent, 2014

YEAR	TEAM	LVL	AGE	W	L	SV	G	GS	IP	H	HR	BB/9	K/9	K	GB%	BABIP
2018	PMB	HI-A	21	1	0	3	8	0	9^2	9	0	1.9	6.5	7	42.9%	.321
2018	SPR	AA	21	0	0	0	16	0	21	19	1	6.9	7.3	17	35.5%	.295
2019	PMB	HI-A	22	0	0	4	9	0	11^2	8	0	6.2	8.5	11	45.2%	.258
2019	SPR	AA	22	1	1	5	18	0	29	18	0	3.4	13.0	42	44.3%	.295
2019	MEM	AAA	22	2	1	2	18	0	24^1	17	0	4.1	10.0	27	62.9%	.274
2019	STL	MLB	22	0	1	0	13	0	11^2	9	2	4.6	12.3	16	50.0%	.269
2020	STL	MLB	23	0	0	0	3	0	3	6	1	6.0	6.0	2	33.3%	.455
2021 FS	*STL*	*MLB*	*24*	*2*	*3*	*0*	*57*	*0*	*50*	*47*	*7*	*6.4*	*9.1*	*50*	*44.2%*	*.293*
2021 DC	*STL*	*MLB*	*24*	*1*	*1*	*0*	*28*	*0*	*29.3*	*27*	*4*	*6.4*	*9.1*	*29*	*44.2%*	*.293*

Comparables: Victor Arano, Jonathan Hernández, Julio Urías

The government will stipulate that Fernández has a triple-digit fastball suited for high-leverage innings if the defense will concede there is not yet enough evidence to convict his slider or changeup of aiding and abetting.

YEAR	TEAM	LVL	AGE	WHIP	ERA	DRA-	WARP	MPH	FB%	WHF	CSP
2018	PMB	HI-A	21	1.14	0.00	68	0.2				
2018	SPR	AA	21	1.67	5.14	93	0.1				
2019	PMB	HI-A	22	1.37	1.54	93	0.0				
2019	SPR	AA	22	1.00	1.55	62	0.6				
2019	MEM	AAA	22	1.15	1.48	48	0.9				
2019	STL	MLB	22	1.29	5.40	68	0.3	98.7	41.7%	43.4%	
2020	STL	MLB	23	2.67	18.00	101	0.0	96.3	55.7%	20.0%	
2021 FS	*STL*	*MLB*	*24*	*1.65*	*5.47*	*117*	*-0.2*	*98.0*	*45.9%*	*36.5%*	*41.2%*
2021 DC	*STL*	*MLB*	*24*	*1.65*	*5.47*	*117*	*-0.1*	*98.0*	*45.9%*	*36.5%*	*41.2%*

St. Louis Cardinals 2021

John Gant RHP
Born: 08/06/92   Age: 28   Bats: R   Throws: R
Height: 6'4"   Weight: 200   Origin: Round 21, 2011 Draft (#642 overall)

YEAR	TEAM	LVL	AGE	W	L	SV	G	GS	IP	H	HR	BB/9	K/9	K	GB%	BABIP
2018	MEM	AAA	25	5	1	0	8	8	49	45	5	2.9	7.7	42	47.9%	.290
2018	STL	MLB	25	7	6	0	26	19	114	91	9	4.5	7.5	95	44.4%	.255
2019	STL	MLB	26	11	1	3	64	0	66.1	51	4	4.6	8.1	60	46.3%	.275
2020	STL	MLB	27	0	3	0	17	0	15	9	0	4.2	10.8	18	63.9%	.250
2021 FS	STL	MLB	28	2	2	0	57	0	50	43	5	3.8	9.2	51	47.8%	.284
2021 DC	STL	MLB	28	2	2	0	50	0	52.7	46	6	3.8	9.2	54	47.8%	.284

Comparables: Robert Stephenson, Joe Musgrove, Matt Wisler

As the 2020 season wore on you could hear the phrase more and more, muttered by despondent batters as they shuffled aimlessly towards the dugout: "Who is John Gant?" He is a shadowy figure with impressively high walk and strikeout rates, the Two True Outcomes most expressive of his individualism; home runs were completely avoided, as they would unjustly reward spectators with souvenirs they have not themselves produced. As for those copious groundball outs, they are most assuredly not a form of collectivism; Gant creates them, his infielders merely cogs in a machine to collect and dispose as per his implicit design. Fluent in five pitches, objectively productive and occasionally dominant, Gant does more than merely earn his keep in a big-league bullpen; he thrives.

YEAR	TEAM	LVL	AGE	WHIP	ERA	DRA-	WARP	MPH	FB%	WHF	CSP
2018	MEM	AAA	25	1.24	1.65	66	1.3				
2018	STL	MLB	25	1.30	3.47	90	1.6	95.4	55.4%	26.4%	
2019	STL	MLB	26	1.28	3.66	88	0.7	97.9	55.7%	27.4%	
2020	STL	MLB	27	1.07	2.40	73	0.3	95.8	52.3%	32.7%	
2021 FS	STL	MLB	28	1.30	3.63	88	0.6	96.6	55.0%	27.8%	48.6%
2021 DC	STL	MLB	28	1.30	3.63	88	0.7	96.6	55.0%	27.8%	48.6%

Tink Hence RHP
Born: 08/06/02   Age: 18   Bats: R   Throws: R
Height: 6'1"   Weight: 175   Origin: Round 2, 2020 Draft (#63 overall)

One of St. Louis' second-round picks, Hence displayed a lightning-fast arm, potential mid-90s heat and three usable secondaries despite being young for his Arkansas prep class; it should go without saying his is a name to remember.

Jordan Hicks   RHP

Born: 09/06/96   Age: 24   Bats: R   Throws: R
Height: 6'2"   Weight: 220   Origin: Round SUP, 2015 Draft (#105 overall)

YEAR	TEAM	LVL	AGE	W	L	SV	G	GS	IP	H	HR	BB/9	K/9	K	GB%	BABIP
2018	STL	MLB	21	3	4	6	73	0	77^2	59	2	5.2	8.1	70	60.6%	.266
2019	STL	MLB	22	2	2	14	29	0	28^2	16	2	3.5	9.7	31	67.2%	.215
2021 FS	STL	MLB	24	2	3	3	57	0	50	46	4	5.9	9.2	50	56.9%	.301
2021 DC	STL	MLB	24	1	1	3	28	0	46.7	43	4	5.9	9.2	47	56.9%	.301

Comparables: Daniel Norris, Sandy Alcantara, Miguel Castro

Hicks was already slated to miss most of last year recovering from Tommy John surgery before COVID-19 hit. Given the young flamethrower's diabetes, he wisely decided to reduce the potential of adding serious illness to injury by opting out of the 2020 season. Hicks is best known for lobbing triple-digit thunderbolts, but when we last saw him on a big-league mound he was flashing an improved slider and better control. Big-league hitters sitting dead-red can turn around anyone's fastball with a quickness, so Hicks' ability to fool them with spin will determine whether or not he can grow into a truly dominant closer. He's only 24, so time and raw talent are on his side.

YEAR	TEAM	LVL	AGE	WHIP	ERA	DRA-	WARP	MPH	FB%	WHF	CSP
2018	STL	MLB	21	1.34	3.59	134	-1.0	103.0	78.0%	24.4%	
2019	STL	MLB	22	0.94	3.14	66	0.7	103.5	60.3%	30.8%	
2021 FS	STL	MLB	24	1.58	4.81	106	0.1	103.2	70.8%	27.0%	46.6%
2021 DC	STL	MLB	24	1.58	4.81	106	0.1	103.2	70.8%	27.0%	46.6%

Rob Kaminsky   LHP

Born: 09/02/94   Age: 26   Bats: R   Throws: L
Height: 6'0"   Weight: 195   Origin: Round 1, 2013 Draft (#28 overall)

YEAR	TEAM	LVL	AGE	W	L	SV	G	GS	IP	H	HR	BB/9	K/9	K	GB%	BABIP
2018	AKR	AA	23	1	1	4	23	0	26^1	22	2	6.2	7.5	22	70.7%	.274
2019	AKR	AA	24	2	1	1	19	0	31^1	22	2	2.3	8.6	30	57.1%	.244
2019	COL	AAA	24	1	0	1	23	0	24^2	26	3	5.1	11.3	31	56.7%	.359
2020	STL	MLB	25	0	0	0	5	0	4^2	3	0	3.9	5.8	3	60.0%	.200
2021 FS	STL	MLB	26	2	2	0	57	0	50	46	5	4.7	8.1	45	53.3%	.282

Comparables: Brady Lail, Alex Reyes, Chase De Jong

After eight years, ligament replacement surgery and a round trip to Cleveland, it took a global pandemic to bring Kaminsky to the St. Louis bullpen. His brief but solid debut may give him a chance to stick around a while.

St. Louis Cardinals 2021

YEAR	TEAM	LVL	AGE	WHIP	ERA	DRA-	WARP	MPH	FB%	WHF	CSP
2018	AKR	AA	23	1.52	3.08	110	-0.1				
2019	AKR	AA	24	0.96	2.30	79	0.3				
2019	COL	AAA	24	1.62	5.11	98	0.3				
2020	STL	MLB	25	1.07	1.93	94	0.1	93.0	42.9%	17.6%	
2021 FS	STL	MLB	26	1.44	4.32	100	0.2	93.0	42.9%	17.6%	44.2%

Matthew Liberatore LHP

Born: 11/06/99   Age: 21   Bats: L   Throws: L
Height: 6'4"   Weight: 200   Origin: Round 1, 2018 Draft (#16 overall)

YEAR	TEAM	LVL	AGE	W	L	SV	G	GS	IP	H	HR	BB/9	K/9	K	GB%	BABIP
2018	RAY	ROK	18	1	2	0	8	8	27^2	16	0	3.6	10.4	32	45.2%	.258
2018	PRN	ROK	18	1	0	0	1	1	5	5	0	3.6	9.0	5	41.7%	.417
2019	BG	LO-A	19	6	2	0	16	15	78^1	70	2	3.6	8.7	76	55.7%	.312
2021 FS	STL	MLB	21	2	3	0	57	0	50	47	7	5.3	7.9	44	47.4%	.282

Comparables: Brailyn Marquez, Randall Delgado, Tyler Chatwood

Randy Arozarena's rocket ride to postseason glory last year has put unfair pressure on both Liberatore (the man he was traded for) to grow into an ace and on the Cardinals (the team who made the trade) to help Liberatore do so as soon as possible. Luckily for everyone involved, Liberatore might just have the goods. A surprisingly polished prep lefty, Liberatore has a tall frame and a clean delivery, and he can hit the mid-90s with his fastball before uncorking knee-buckling benders that could eventually rank among the league's best. Without a new minor-league season to overwrite them, Liberatore's mundane strikeout numbers as a teenager in the Midwest League are still a gnawing concern to some but team officials (surprise!) raved about his development at their Springfield complex over the summer. Liberatore has a high floor, and, if Uncle Charlie grows into a true wipeout offering, he could one day front a rotation.

YEAR	TEAM	LVL	AGE	WHIP	ERA	DRA-	WARP	MPH	FB%	WHF	CSP
2018	RAY	ROK	18	0.98	0.98						
2018	PRN	ROK	18	1.40	3.60						
2019	BG	LO-A	19	1.29	3.10	98	0.4				
2021 FS	STL	MLB	21	1.53	5.00	112	-0.1				

Miles Mikolas RHP

Born: 08/23/88 Age: 32 Bats: R Throws: R
Height: 6'4" Weight: 230 Origin: Round 7, 2009 Draft (#204 overall)

YEAR	TEAM	LVL	AGE	W	L	SV	G	GS	IP	H	HR	BB/9	K/9	K	GB%	BABIP
2018	STL	MLB	29	18	4	0	32	32	200^2	186	16	1.3	6.5	146	48.1%	.282
2019	STL	MLB	30	9	14	0	32	32	184	193	27	1.6	7.0	144	47.4%	.304
2021 FS	STL	MLB	32	10	7	0	26	26	150	147	18	1.7	7.2	120	47.4%	.288
2021 DC	STL	MLB	32	7	6	0	19	21	113.7	111	14	1.7	7.2	91	47.4%	.288

Comparables: Dan Straily, Kyle Hendricks, Heath Hembree

Doctors often ask overweight middle-aged men to address their high blood pressure through diet and exercise in order to avoid medication; this rarely works, since there's a reason they are overweight middle-aged men in the first place. Similarly, attempts to treat a pitcher's sore elbow with platelet rich plasma injections often seem to merely delay the inevitable date with the knife. Mikolas went the PRP route after reporting to spring training with a forearm strain, hoping he could be ready for the season's delayed July start. He wasn't, and subsequent surgery on his flexor tendon caused him to miss all of 2020. He should be ready for spring training, assuming spring training is ready for him, and if he's healthy there's no reason Mikolas shouldn't be able to settle back into the middle of the Cardinals rotation.

YEAR	TEAM	LVL	AGE	WHIP	ERA	DRA-	WARP	MPH	FB%	WHF	CSP
2018	STL	MLB	29	1.07	2.83	75	4.5	96.1	48.6%	20.3%	
2019	STL	MLB	30	1.22	4.16	84	3.3	95.6	51.4%	21.8%	
2021 FS	STL	MLB	32	1.17	3.44	86	2.6	95.8	50.4%	21.3%	49.7%
2021 DC	STL	MLB	32	1.17	3.44	86	2.0	95.8	50.4%	21.3%	49.7%

St. Louis Cardinals 2021

Roel Ramirez RHP
Born: 05/26/95   Age: 26   Bats: R   Throws: R
Height: 6'0"   Weight: 235   Origin: Round 8, 2013 Draft (#248 overall)

YEAR	TEAM	LVL	AGE	W	L	SV	G	GS	IP	H	HR	BB/9	K/9	K	GB%	BABIP
2018	CHA	HI-A	23	0	0	1	8	0	12^2	4	0	0.0	9.9	14	53.6%	.143
2018	SPR	AA	23	0	0	0	10	0	10^2	8	1	4.2	8.4	10	35.7%	.259
2018	MTG	AA	23	3	1	0	26	1	40^2	37	4	3.8	10.2	46	35.5%	.320
2019	SPR	AA	24	5	3	1	41	5	72^1	76	6	3.6	10.0	80	40.0%	.363
2020	STL	MLB	25	0	0	0	1	0	0^2	6	4	13.5	13.5	1	33.3%	1.000
2021 FS	STL	MLB	26	2	3	0	57	0	50	49	8	3.7	8.8	48	38.2%	.297

Comparables: James Norwood, Madison Younginer, Dovydas Neverauskas

Ramirez made one appearance last season and is now the only player in major league history to allow four or more home runs while retiring one or fewer batters in his career. If the Cardinals never give him another chance to wash away that regret, they should at least give him a Burt Lancaster mustache, pay for medical school and set him up in a small-town practice outside Laredo.

YEAR	TEAM	LVL	AGE	WHIP	ERA	DRA-	WARP	MPH	FB%	WHF	CSP
2018	CHA	HI-A	23	0.32	0.00	77	0.2				
2018	SPR	AA	23	1.22	5.06	53	0.3				
2018	MTG	AA	23	1.33	3.32	77	0.6				
2019	SPR	AA	24	1.45	4.98	105	-0.4				
2020	STL	MLB	25	10.50	81.00	122	0.0	94.4	63.3%	21.4%	
2021 FS	STL	MLB	26	1.41	4.79	110	-0.1	94.4	63.3%	21.4%	44.8%

Ricardo Sánchez LHP
Born: 04/11/97   Age: 24   Bats: L   Throws: L
Height: 5'10"   Weight: 220   Origin: International Free Agent, 2013

YEAR	TEAM	LVL	AGE	W	L	SV	G	GS	IP	H	HR	BB/9	K/9	K	GB%	BABIP
2018	DAN	ROK	21	1	0	0	2	2	11^2	11	1	2.3	6.9	9	54.1%	.278
2018	MIS	AA	21	2	5	0	13	13	57^2	65	3	3.7	6.9	44	40.7%	.333
2019	ARK	AA	22	8	12	0	27	27	146	157	10	2.3	8.3	135	48.5%	.349
2020	STL	MLB	23	0	0	0	3	0	5^1	5	1	8.4	6.8	4	35.3%	.250
2021 FS	STL	MLB	24	2	3	0	57	0	50	49	7	4.8	7.5	41	43.6%	.286

Comparables: Justus Sheffield, Génesis Cabrera, Beau Burrows

Let's hope well-traveled lefty Sánchez can smile when he remembers the high heat he blew past Ian Happ for his first career punchout last August; he'll need all the positive vibes he can muster while he rehabs from offseason elbow surgery.

YEAR	TEAM	LVL	AGE	WHIP	ERA	DRA-	WARP	MPH	FB%	WHF	CSP
2018	DAN	ROK	21	1.20	3.09						
2018	MIS	AA	21	1.54	4.06	134	-0.7				
2019	ARK	AA	22	1.34	4.44	116	-1.2				
2020	STL	MLB	23	1.88	6.75	123	0.0	92.9	49.6%	23.5%	
2021 FS	STL	MLB	24	1.53	5.09	114	-0.2	92.9	49.6%	23.5%	41.0%

Zack Thompson LHP

Born: 10/28/97   Age: 23   Bats: L   Throws: L
Height: 6'2"   Weight: 215   Origin: Round 1, 2019 Draft (#19 overall)

YEAR	TEAM	LVL	AGE	W	L	SV	G	GS	IP	H	HR	BB/9	K/9	K	GB%	BABIP
2019	CAR	ROK	21	0	0	0	2	2	2	3	0	0.0	18.0	4	66.7%	.500
2019	PMB	HI-A	21	0	0	0	11	0	13.1	16	0	2.7	12.8	19	48.6%	.471
2021 FS	STL	MLB	23	2	3	0	57	0	50	47	7	4.3	8.5	47	42.4%	.287

Comparables: Julio Urías, Jesús Luzardo, Ryan Perry

With no minor-league season last year, pitching prospects lost the irreplaceable opportunity to hone their craft in game situations against hundreds of different batters. Of course, spending the summer in the controlled environment of a team's alternate site allowed them avoid the wear and tear of travel and lessened the chance of incidental injury. On balance, that might have been a good thing for Thompson, a high-floor, low-ceiling lefty with four quality pitchers but none that scream plus-plus. He suffered through arm problems in both high school and college and he wasn't exactly babied in his years at the University of Kentucky, so leaving a little more tread on the tires last year may make it more likely the development staff will eventually deliver him to the middle of the Cardinals rotation safe and sound.

YEAR	TEAM	LVL	AGE	WHIP	ERA	DRA-	WARP	MPH	FB%	WHF	CSP
2019	CAR	ROK	21	1.50	0.00						
2019	PMB	HI-A	21	1.50	4.05	137	-0.3				
2021 FS	STL	MLB	23	1.43	4.79	111	-0.1				

Kodi Whitley RHP

Born: 02/21/95 Age: 26 Bats: R Throws: R
Height: 6'3" Weight: 220 Origin: Round 27, 2017 Draft (#814 overall)

YEAR	TEAM	LVL	AGE	W	L	SV	G	GS	IP	H	HR	BB/9	K/9	K	GB%	BABIP
2018	PEO	LO-A	23	4	2	9	41	2	71^2	67	2	3.3	8.5	68	45.4%	.322
2019	PMB	HI-A	24	0	0	0	3	0	4^1	1	0	4.2	10.4	5	37.5%	.125
2019	SPR	AA	24	1	4	7	31	0	39^1	31	3	3.0	10.5	46	40.0%	.277
2019	MEM	AAA	24	2	0	2	16	0	23^2	21	0	1.5	10.3	27	27.7%	.323
2020	STL	MLB	25	0	0	0	4	0	4^2	2	1	1.9	9.6	5	36.4%	.100
2021 FS	STL	MLB	26	2	2	0	57	0	50	46	8	2.5	8.9	49	36.4%	.283
2021 DC	STL	MLB	26	1	1	0	39	0	46.7	43	7	2.5	8.9	46	36.4%	.283

Comparables: Cody Ege, Wei-Chieh Huang, Colton Murray

Time spent successfully recovering from COVID-19 and a sore elbow limited Whitley to four appearances in his Cardinals debut, but the strapping young right-hander showed enough to earn a spot on the team's playoff roster and future plans. His four-seamer sat in the mid-90s but he can reach back for more when he needs it, his changeup and slider both miss bats and unlike so many other live-armed relief prospects he avoids ball four. Gopher balls will be an intermittent problem for him but Whitley has the stuff to headline a major-league bullpen; if that doesn't pan out, he has the name to headline a major pop tour.

YEAR	TEAM	LVL	AGE	WHIP	ERA	DRA-	WARP	MPH	FB%	WHF	CSP
2018	PEO	LO-A	23	1.30	2.51	72	1.3				
2019	PMB	HI-A	24	0.69	0.00	63	0.1				
2019	SPR	AA	24	1.12	1.83	57	0.9				
2019	MEM	AAA	24	1.06	1.52	45	0.9				
2020	STL	MLB	25	0.64	1.93	95	0.1	95.1	53.2%	33.3%	
2021 FS	STL	MLB	26	1.21	3.74	92	0.5	95.1	53.2%	33.3%	45.7%
2021 DC	STL	MLB	26	1.21	3.74	92	0.4	95.1	53.2%	33.3%	45.7%

Cardinals Prospects

The State of the System:
A combination of power bats, intriguing close-to-ready arms, and marginal depth all adds up to an averagish system.

The Top Ten:

1

★ ★ ★ *2021 Top 101 Prospect* **#16** ★ ★ ★

Dylan Carlson RF   OFP: 70   ETA: Debuted in 2020
Born: 10/23/98   Age: 22   Bats: S   Throws: L   Height: 6'2"   Weight: 205
Origin: Round 1, 2016 Draft (#33 overall)

The Report: A 2016 draftee who was young for his class, Carlson showed flashes of the five-tool outfield prospect he would become during aggressive A-ball assignments in 2017 and 2018, but a combination of seeing a lot of older, more experienced arms, and some brutal hitting environments meant the overall line somewhat underwhelmed. It all clicked for Carlson in 2019, as he torched the upper minors, making notable improvements to his power stroke and his quick-twitch speed—leading to an above-average center field glove projection after barely playing there the previous two years—and he established himself as a top 20 prospect in baseball. Carlson does everything well, a potential plus hit/power center fielder with a solid approach, who has the foot speed and arm to play any of the three outfield spots.

Development Track: Carlson got a shot at regular playing time early in 2020 as the Cardinals dealt with a COVID-19 outbreak. The early returns were better than the top line stats, as he took good at-bats and hit the ball hard, but lined some balls right at defenders and ended up with a few too many Ks running those deep counts. Carlson hit the reset button back at the alternate site, and blistered the ball after coming back up for the last few weeks of the season. He started for the Cardinals in the playoffs and looks to be a starting outfielder for them going forward. The overall line doesn't look amazing for a major league debut, but going forward we'd expect him to be closer to the .800 OPS he posted in September.

St. Louis Cardinals 2021

Variance: Medium. If we were still doing OFP/Likely, I think the likely 60 outcome here is pretty stable, given the broad base of skills and adjustments Carlson has made already in the majors. He will have to fine tune the hit tool and approach to get to the All-Star level, though, and those last little skill jumps in the majors can be the hardest.

Mark Barry's Fantasy Take: It was a disappointing 2020 for Carlson, but it was a disappointing 2020 for me too, so who am I to judge? I'm not sure much has changed since this time last year. Maybe the ceiling is slightly lower, but the floor is still pretty high, as is the potential for five-category impact.

──────── ★ ★ ★ *2021 Top 101 Prospect* **#23** ★ ★ ★ ────────

2. Nolan Gorman   3B   OFP: 60   ETA: Late 2021/Early 2022
Born: 05/10/00   Age: 21   Bats: L   Throws: R   Height: 6'1"   Weight: 210
Origin: Round 1, 2018 Draft (#19 overall)

The Report: Gorman's pre-draft buzz had him among the top prep bats in 2018, but concerns about hit hit tool and ultimate defensive home caused him to slide to the 19th pick. He responded by destroying the Appalachian League in June and July, earning a full-season assignment a scant few months after his 18th birthday. The power continued to show up in A-ball in 2019, and it's true elite raw with potential 30+ home run seasons to come once Gorman hones his approach against better pitching. The strikeouts also piled up against A-ball pitching, and he does take Paul Bunyan-esque cuts at the ball, so he may never show better than an average hit tool. The defense has consistently looked average at the hot corner as a pro, and given how filled out Gorman already is, there's less concern he will grow off the position. It's not a lock though, and he's unlikely to be much better than a tick above-average there. That's fine as long as the thunder in the bat is as loud as we expect.

Development Track: Gorman was a monster at the plate in March, and looked to be taking another step forward this spring before the shutdown. After cooling his heels for a few months, the alternate site reports were a little more muted. In this case I will defer to the mountain of knowledge we have about the bat that didn't come in the midst of a global pandemic, while granting that the concerns about the hit tool and third base defense will only be dispelled for certain with upper level game action.

Variance: High. There's absolutely All-Star upside here if Gorman can make enough high-quality contact to run some .280+ batting averages. There's also still risk the swing-and-miss eats into the overall line and the third base glove ends up fringy or worse.

Mark Barry's Fantasy Take: It would have been nice to see Gorman finally test himself against advanced-level pitching, but realistically the only question left for the former-first rounder is whether he'll hit for enough contact to be a fantasy stud. The power is legit and could lead to plenty of 30+ homer campaigns, but the average will be the deciding factor as to whether those dingers will be empty or not.

★ ★ ★ 2021 Top 101 Prospect #43 ★ ★ ★

3 **Matthew Liberatore** **LHP** OFP: 60 ETA: 2022
Born: 11/06/99 Age: 21 Bats: L Throws: L Height: 6'4" Weight: 200
Origin: Round 1, 2018 Draft (#16 overall)

The Report: Liberatore had top-10 pick buzz going into the 2018 draft as a tall, projectable prep lefty with feel for spin. His height gives him good extension and plane on a fastball with above-average velocity for a southpaw, although the command is more on the fringy side. His best secondary is an 11-6 curve that comes from a tough angle and might have enough late action to miss bats at the highest level. Like most prep pitching prospects, the change was a developmental need, but he has solid, if inconsistent feel for it already.

Development Track: Well, Liberatore looks more or less like the same good lefty pitching prospect with advanced feel for spin. The trade that brought him to St. Louis looks a little bit different though. Obviously we won't hold that against him, but the lost year of game reps hurts a bit. Liberatore was at the alternate site and could start 2021 in Double-A, so he might not be that far off the majors himself, but we'll be looking for a more obvious out pitch against upper minors bats in 2021.

Variance: Medium. Liberatore has never really "felt" like a prep prospect, as he's been more polish than stuff—and I suppose is now roughly college junior age. There's the outline of four pitches, some feel for the change. The command outcome here will dictate if there's upside past mid-rotation, or if he's more of a backend guy. There's been some arm worries in the past too, but I mean, he's a pitcher.

Mark Barry's Fantasy Take: Without tweaks to his pitch mix or refinement of secondary offerings, Liberatore might be looking at a Marco Gonzales-esque ceiling. And that's not a knock, Gonzales is pretty good—it's just not the most enticing best case scenario. The most likely outcome is that Liberatore turns out to be a back-end starter that hangs around forever because he's a lefty.

★ ★ ★ 2021 Top 101 Prospect #92 ★ ★ ★

4 **Jordan Walker** **3B** OFP: 60 ETA: 2023
Born: 05/22/02 Age: 19 Bats: R Throws: R Height: 6'5" Weight: 220
Origin: Round 1, 2020 Draft (#21 overall)

The Report: Walker offered big power and big upside with a frame that might not allow him to stick at third base long term. Sound familiar? The 6-foot-5 Walker gets to his prodigious raw pop with longer levers than Gorman's, and the swing-and-miss concerns are just as ... well, concerning. There's very few third basemen in the majors who look like him either, just on build, so a move to a corner outfield spot or first base might be in the cards. The arm will play just fine at third base—or in right field for that matter—as Walker was up to 93 off the mound as a prep.

Development Track: We started getting big reports on Walker almost as soon as he landed at the alternate site. He can match Gorman for raw pop and posted elite exit velocities as an 18-year-old seeing far older and more advanced pitching. Gorman had a similar jump post-draft himself, but we'd feel a lot better pushing Walker as hard if those big bombs had come in Appalachian League games in Johnson City rather than the alternate site in Springfield. In the converse of the Gorman situation, we don't want to strap too big of a rocket to Walker until we see it in games—and given how aggressive the Cardinals have been recently with their top prospect bats, that could be in Advanced-A in 2021—but maybe we can attach a little V2 to the 21st overall pick, as a treat.

Variance: Extreme. It's easy to get ahead of yourself a bit with this kind of player doing these kinds of things against far more advanced pitching. We do still want to see how the swing plays against more age-appropriate pitching in real games. This could be a bit of a slow burn with a prospect track that requires some patience.

Mark Barry's Fantasy Take: "CTRL C" the Gorman analysis, but add a longer timeline and probably a final destination in the outfield. There's a lot to dream on with Walker, but we've literally seen nothing yet.

5 Zack Thompson   LHP   OFP: 55   ETA: 2021 as a reliever / 2022 or later as a starter
Born: 10/28/97   Age: 23   Bats: L   Throws: L   Height: 6'2"   Weight: 215
Origin: Round 1, 2019 Draft (#19 overall)

The Report: When you've been as competitive as the Cardinals have been for the better part of a generation—just one losing season in the last 20 years—and Major League Baseball operates the amateur draft with a reverse record order, it's tough to get really good players. Yet, somehow and some way they snag guys like Thompson, who for one reason or another fall into their laps. In this particular case, despite having probably the best stuff of any college pitcher in the 2019 draft, Thompson slid because of durability concerns as a starter. Using a mid-90s heater that has good wiggle to it, he has a very deceptive arm action that hides his intended pitch selection, which also includes a hard-biting breaking ball and steady changeup.

Development Track: Past arm injuries will always put into question the possibility of a reliever profile, especially as Thompson has done when deployed as a reliever. The stuff and frame are plenty good to start, no denying that's where you keep running him out every fifth day for as long as possible. If the decision is made he'll hold up better in the bullpen, he could be fast-tracked very quickly to the majors.

Variance: High. Until he can show a full season of starting the confidence level associated with the reliever risk is too much to ignore.

Mark Barry's Fantasy Take: It wouldn't surprise me if Thompson was up in 2021 and was pretty good. It also wouldn't surprise me if he comes up and gets rocked. It also wouldn't surprise me if sometimes he was good and sometimes he was bad. And it also wouldn't surprise me if he got hurt again, as he has been wont to do. The mean outcome for all these possibilities is that Thompson is decent, and worth rostering in 200+ prospect leagues, but I'm not sure if the ceiling is super high.

6 Ivan Herrera   C   OFP: 55   ETA: Late 2021/Early 2022
Born: 06/01/00   Age: 21   Bats: R   Throws: R   Height: 5'11"   Weight: 220
Origin: International Free Agent, 2016

The Report: The latest in a long line of catching prospects stuck behind Yadier Molina, Herrera doesn't have Andrew Knizner's upside with the bat nor Carson Kelly's with the glove, but there's no real weakness in his game either. The hit tool is ahead of the power, although he will show some pullside pop, but his short stroke and feel for contact should play against better velocity. He's still developing behind the plate, but Herrera is a sure shot catcher who is average or above-average at all aspects of backstop defense.

Development Track: With Molina set to hit free agency post-2020, you would have liked to see Herrera establish himself in the upper minors and put himself in position to win the job at some point in 2021. Instead, he was one of the Cardinals' six catchers at their alternate site where he didn't do anything to dissuade us from his above-average projection or stake his claim to the long term catching job. There's always 2021.

Variance: High. Catchers are weird.

Mark Barry's Fantasy Take: I want to pitch a Succession-like show, but the objective is not to take over a multimedia conglomerate, but to be the next starting catcher for the St. Louis Cardinals. Molina is in a coma and Knizner and Herrera vie to take the throne. And for some reason, Kelly is there too. Herrera could be an above-average fantasy catcher, but in one-catcher leagues, I'm not sure that means much.

7 Johan Oviedo   RHP   OFP: 55   ETA: Debuted in 2020
Born: 03/02/98   Age: 23   Bats: R   Throws: R   Height: 6'5"   Weight: 245
Origin: International Free Agent, 2016

The Report: Oviedo is a big dude who throws mostly power stuff and comes at you from a difficult angle due to his extension and arm slot. His best offering is his heavy mid-90s fastball, which touched 99 mph in the majors this season. His primary offspeed is a hard slider that sits in the mid-80s and has improved greatly. The slider looks like a second above-average-to-plus pitch now. The issues here are command and whether he can find a usable third pitch. Oviedo doesn't always throw enough strikes, and sometimes when he is hitting the zone he's missing within the zone, dead red when he needs to hit a corner. He throws both a changeup and curveball, but the change is too firm and the curve is too soft at present. There's significant relief risk present unless something jumps.

Development Track: Oviedo was impressive enough during summer camp and at the alternate site that he got called up to make five starts down the stretch. He was pretty bad, and frankly he probably wasn't ready to be in the majors. But the fastball and slider were there, and he threw more strikes than he had in the minors.

Variance: Medium. He could really use a jump in a secondary offering or command, but he's already made the majors and there's an obvious bullpen fallback with the fastball and slider.

Mark Barry's Fantasy Take: This profile feels very reliever-y, so Oviedo doesn't need to be on your radar until the day he takes over ninth-inning duties (which also might not happen).

8 Masyn Winn SS
Born: 03/21/02 Age: 19 Bats: R Throws: R Height: 5'11" Weight: 180
Origin: Round 2, 2020 Draft (#54 overall)

The Report: The old football adage, "if you have two quarterbacks, you really have none," is similar in baseball when speaking of two-way players. Contemporary players have become so specialized to harness their best attributes that most often those who actually try to both hit and pitch usually struggle to advance quickly in either. With all that said, Winn actually might have a shot at succeeding at both. At one of the biggest amateur scouting events in Jupiter, Fla., he cruised at 93-95, topping out at 97 with feel to spin some nasty breaking balls. In that same game, he crushed a monster home run into the wind. Every indication from the Cardinals suggest he will be developed simultaneously on the mound and at shortstop.

Development Track: He lacks the ideal size you want to see out of a typical starting pitcher, appearing more like a prototypical shortstop. Maintaining his body to contribute every day he will have to work on building the best base possible in his legs. Watch him being brought along slowly to give every aspect of his game time to grow.

Variance: Extreme. Will it work? Who knows. Maybe he'll have to give up one or the other at some point. The success stories are so rare it's hard to project in the most optimistic terms where it will end up.

Mark Barry's Fantasy Take: Clearly as a middle infielder/pitcher prospect, Winn's pedigree is reminiscent of, uh, well, it's a bit of a current anomaly. The idea that the Cardinals are going to develop him as a two-way player further muddies the dynasty waters. And that's totally fine, it's just hard to gauge how good/valuable he'll be until we see the development in practice. Winn is a fine dart throw, and maybe even a good one, but that's all he is right now.

9. Kodi Whitley   RHP   OFP: 50   ETA: Debuted in 2020
Born: 02/21/95   Age: 26   Bats: R   Throws: R   Height: 6'3"   Weight: 220
Origin: Round 27, 2017 Draft (#814 overall)

The Report: Whitely always dominated in the minors, but as a 27th round redshirt junior with a Tommy John in college, the Cardinals didn't exactly push him as aggressively as some of the more notable names higher up the list. He forced the issue in 2019 though as a velocity bump into the upper-90s, paired with his plus slider, caused him to blitz three levels and left him on the doorstep of a major league bullpen role. Whitley is not just a two-pitch reliever either, as the changeup has some utility due to the deception from his arm speed.

Development Track: Whitely's pop-up velocity didn't entirely stick, as he was more of a 95-and-a-slider guy in his brief major league stint than an upper-90s-and-a-slider guy. He did deal with a minor elbow injury which might explain some of that, but also is a little concerning on its own. The slider was as advertised though, mid-80s with late, tight break. The straight change looked pretty good as well. Whitely could use those couple extra ticks back on the fastball to have true end of game utility, but he should slot in as a useful setup level reliever regardless.

Variance: Low. Whitley is ready for a major league bullpen role right now. How good the fastball is going forward will determine which inning he's utilized in however.

Mark Barry's Fantasy Take: Whitley got a bunch of whiffs in an abbreviated stint with the big club in 2020, but didn't see many high-leverage innings. His ideal role might be as a bulk reliever, which is only useful in the deepest of leagues.

10. Tink Hence   RHP   OFP: 50   ETA: 2025
Born: 08/06/02   Age: 18   Bats: R   Throws: R   Height: 6'1"   Weight: 175
Origin: Round 2, 2020 Draft (#63 overall)

The Report: Go down the list of things you want when drafting a prep pitching prospect and Hence would satisfy nearly every quality required. Except for one, but we'll get to that later. From an athletic, repeatable, and balanced delivery, the ball explodes out of his hand. Sitting in the low 90s at present, he's touched 95 on occasion with late life that also explains the late finish to his breaking ball. The arm swing and athletic control of his body through release make him a perfectly suitable Comp B round pick to dream on.

Development Track: Why not higher? Everything sounded great above, there must be a catch. Truth is: he's very skinny, with a frame that won't likely allow for much gains in the strength department. Stamina and durability might also creep into concerns without the usual mass needed to sustain a long season.

Variance: Very High. There's a lot to like to go along with the hard-to-forget barriers.

Mark Barry's Fantasy Take: I'm not writing off an 18-year-old kid, but until he can find a reliable third pitch, he's probably a reliever.

The Prospects You Meet Outside The Top Ten

Interesting 2020 Draft Follows

Alec Burleson Born: 11/25/98 Age: 22 Bats: L Throws: L Height: 6'2" Weight: 212 Origin: Round 2, 2020 Draft (#70 overall)

Another two-way player? Unlikely, even though Burleson starred at East Carolina University as one of the better ones in the country. His path to the big leagues is as a position player with a bat-first profile. With an arm that is serviceable off the mound (future blowout position player pitching?) you'd think he'd be a surefire right fielder to let the arm play up, however his lack of mobility probably relegates him to left field or first base. There is some decent barrel control and a line-drive swing that provides enough carry to get some of his raw power.

Ian Bedell Born: 09/05/99 Age: 21 Bats: R Throws: R Height: 6'2" Weight: 198 Origin: Round 4, 2020 Draft (#122 overall)

A trendy name in the 2020 draft thanks to a lights-out Cape performance, there is still a great deal unknown to his game thanks to his very short track record as a starter. In fact, he started more in the Cape than he had in his previous two years at Mizzou. A very repeatable and consistent delivery that allows for maximum strike-throwing lifts an overall average repertoire into something a bit more interesting than Bedell's typically would suggest. Along with a low-90s fastball he shows a curve that has some plus qualities to it and a cutter and changeup. Throw in the Cardinals player dev(il) magic, and the fuzzy picture of a back-end starter begins to take focus.

Prospects to dream on a little

Edwin Nunez RHP Born: 11/05/01 Age: 19 Bats: R Throws: R Height: 6'3" Weight: 185 Origin: International Free Agent, 2019

Signed last summer at 18 for $525,000 after having to sit out due to a misrepresented age, Nuñez has regularly been hitting triple digits—and not stopping at 100. He's mostly just an arm strength prospect at this point, but it's a lot of arm strength and he still has some room to fill out further.

MLB bats, but less upside than you'd like

Evan Mendoza 3B Born: 06/28/96 Age: 25 Bats: R Throws: R Height: 6'2" Weight: 200 Origin: Round 11, 2017 Draft (#334 overall)

Mendoza has never really recaptured his Top Ten system shine whether it was injury or the bat stagnating some in the upper minors, or both. But even though the average raw power might never really play in games, there's still enough of a hit tool and defensive flexibility to make him a useful utility type.

Top Talents 25 and Under (as of 4/1/2021):

1. Jack Flaherty, RHP
2. Dylan Carlson, OF
3. Nolan Gorman, 3B
4. Matthew Liberatore, LHP
5. Jordan Walker, 3B
6. Zack Thompson, LHP
7. Tommy Edman, IF/OF
8. Ivan Herrera, C
9. Johan Oviedo, RHP
10. Masyn Winn, RHP/SS

Sometimes mid-rotation starting prospects become top-of-the-rotation starters. Jack Flaherty wasn't at his best for a lot of 2020, but he still turned in a decent campaign, and in the two seasons before that he was one of the better pitchers in the National League. He's got a big fastball/slider combination he can ride, and he could contend for a Cy Young in any given year.

Tommy Edman was a sensational find for the Cards. He can play nearly anywhere on the field—in just 170 MLB games he's already started more than 10 times at third, second, right field, and short—and he's useful at the plate, even if the power backed up. Cardinals Devil Magic never ends.

Part 3: Featured Articles

Cardinals All-Time Top 10 Players

by Matthew Trueblood

POSITION PLAYERS

TED SIMMONS, C (1968–1980)
Only six post-Deadball Era catchers have gotten at least 300 plate appearances in a season at age 20 or younger. Now that Simmons has been elected to the Hall of Fame, half of the sextet have plaques. More tellingly, Simmons was something almost unheard-of when he debuted: A switch-hitting catcher. Of the 17 ambi-slugging backstops to surpass 2,000 career plate appearances since 1920, only three had appeared when Simmons established himself at the dawn of the 1970s, and two of those had retired before Franklin Roosevelt became President. Simmons was a true switch-hitter, with a near-zero platoon split, and was a fine defender at the game's most demanding position, though this assessment was controversial while he was still active. He also went to bat for the players' rights to earn more money and freedom to choose their teams.

YADIER MOLINA, C (2004–Present)
Our Fielding Runs Above Average data is imperfect for measuring defense throughout baseball history and comparing any modern catcher to players from decades ago using numbers is unfair. Today we can measure and assign value to things that we could only speculate about as recently as 15 years ago. Thus, when we note that Molina has the most FRAA in our database it does not necessarily follow that he's the greatest defensive player of all time or even the greatest defensive catcher. What we can safely say is that the only player who has verifiably saved over 250 runs without being a pitcher. He's also a league-average hitter. Those tangible things evince his greatness. The intangibles—his knack for coming up big in key moments, whatever qualities permit him to get more out of pitchers than most catchers do—make it possible to argue he should rank more highly than even our measurements permit.

STAN MUSIAL, OF/1B (1941–1963)

There were deep scars on Musial's heart from enduring a tough childhood of a coal miner's son during the Great Depression. He never wore them where anyone could see them, though, becoming famous as much for his effervescent enthusiasm and smile as for his unorthodox, coiled batting stance, and as much for those things as for his masterful hitting. Musial had at least 40 doubles and at least 10 triples in five different seasons, two more such campaigns than any other player since 1940. At his 1948 peak he hit .376/.450/.702 with 46 doubles, 18 triples, and 39 home runs. It was about as good a season as anyone has ever had. If his harmonica-playing, grandpa-but-still-playing (by the end he was) persona has overshadowed just how good he was, that's not such a bad legacy to leave posterity.

ALBERT PUJOLS, 1B/OF (2001–2011)

With the 10th anniversary of Pujols's departure for Orange County looming this fall, the number of Cardinals fans who don't even remember him at his best is growing quickly (albeit not as quickly as it might be if baseball were better marketed to the young). From his famously wide, spread-out stance with his hands in a lethal, loaded position behind his ear, he generated extraordinary all-fields power without ever seeming to sacrifice an iota of balance. Those controlled explosions, plus his almost bionic batting eye and peerless baserunning instincts, made him a kind of National League terminator. It was Cardinals general manager Branch Rickey who advised shedding a player a year too early rather than a year too late and his successors were correct to follow his edict with regards to Pujols' 30s, but all these years later it still seems incongruous to see him in an Angels uniform.

ROGERS HORNSBY, 2B (1915–1937)

The best player page at Baseball-Reference might just belong to Hornsby. From 1920-25, no other player led the National League in batting average, on-base percentage, or slugging in any season. He hit .397/.467/.666 in 845 games during those years. His famous quotation about spending the winter longing for spring (and the return of baseball) might be thought of as the understandable itch felt by one so transcendent in their field that they become addicted to it. In truth, alas, it betrayed a real level of aloofness and misanthropy that made him a miserable teammate, and the Cardinals elected to make his personality other people's problem just one year after that famous stretch ended.

KEN BOYER, 3B (1955–1965)

Both in the field and at bat Boyer honed a truly spare style that made him great, though often underrated. He was a late bloomer, partially thanks to being called to service during the Korean War, and thus, he was never among the league's most dynamic pure athletes. Instead, he developed an economy of movement (including saving his swings for hittable pitches) that permitted unusual consistency. From 1958-64, Boyer never posted a DRC+ south of 123, and was never worth fewer than 4.7 WARP.

OZZIE SMITH, SS (1982–1996)
Truly great ballplayers have a way of making the game seem balletic. For pitchers, it's easy: So much of their craft is twisting and craning up on one foot and finishing with a powerful, balanced, graceful flourish. Batters, too, rotate, every limb under control, and strike poses that inspire words far beyond mere descriptions of their actual position. Fielders, though, have to be quick, functional, and efficient. They have to respond to the chaotic collisions of round balls and round bats. Learned baseball watchers know and appreciate great defense, but it's rare that a great play afield shares the objective elegance of the controlled environment that is the batter-pitcher showdown. Smith was the exception that proved the rule: he inspired teams to seek emulators, but none could match him for sheer defensive value or (especially) for beauty.

ENOS SLAUGHTER, OF (1938–1942, 1946–1953)
Slaughter's three years away from MLB during World War II probably cost him a place in the true pantheon of the game. A left-handed hitter with a high-RPM motor, he was a .308/.378/.485 career hitter at the time of his departure for the war. In the eight seasons surrounding his absence, he averaged 173 hits. Give him that many per year (reasonable, since he was gone from ages 27 to 29) for the war years, and he's within 100 career hits of 3,000. Early in his career (and especially in Game 7 of the 1946 World Series), he also added value with his legs, on the bases and in right field.

CURT FLOOD, OF (1956–1969)
Because of his overwhelming importance to the battle for labor rights in baseball it's easy to forget how good Flood was. In a career that functionally spanned just 12 seasons, and in which he came to bat fewer than 7,000 times, he was a 40-win player. Like Willie Davis or Devon White, Flood was an elite defensive center fielder, and while his bat was only average (great contact skills, some speed, but no power or patience), that meant that his glove didn't have to make up for anything. His numbers speak well of him, but long after newer statistical estimations have replaced them, and after his career has faded past the horizon in our rearview mirrors, his words will remain: "I do not feel that I am a piece of property to be bought and sold irrespective of my wishes."

LOU BROCK, OF (1964–1979)
Comparing other great (or non-great) players to Brock is folly. He didn't walk much, and had below-average isolated power, but by trading contact for quality of contact, he sustained a batting average on balls in play 20 percent higher than

an average player of his era and environment. He conceptualized stealing bases, and the application of his speed in general, as an exercise of his power, through the explosion and the force of will that allowed him to succeed that way. The things he did best were the things teams fought hardest to prevent, but through his intellect, tenacity, and tremendous talent, Brock overpowered opponents.

PITCHERS

JESSE HAINES, RHP (1920–1937)

Even in 2021, we run into arguments and gray areas around pitch classification. Haines, though, is a reminder of how relatively clear things are now. What he and many of his contemporaries called his knuckleball—leading him to be lumped in with knuckleballers even today—was, by any modern definition, a slider. Haines only adjusted his four-seam fastball grip by closing his two fingers and pushing the ball in against the inside of his knuckles. By all accounts, it was a devastating pitch, when he had command of it, with a tight vertical drop off the plane of his high heat. Haines was more durable than dominant, though, because his command of the offering was inconsistent. One of many Frankie Frisch-adjacent players elevated to the Hall of Fame by the Veterans Committee which is unfortunate as it focused attention on what Haines was not (an all-time great) instead of what he was (a perfectly cromulent pitcher).

DIZZY DEAN, RHP (1930, 1932–1937)

Don't be fooled by the dates his career technically spanned. Dean actually established himself in 1932, was fighting to stay healthy by 1937, and made multiple appearances in a season for the last time in 1940. From 1932-36, he averaged 34 starts, 15 relief appearances, and 306 innings per year. Doing it that way—pitching that often—made pitching that much inevitably fatal to his arm. He burned bright, though: he won four straight strikeout titles through 1935, carried the Cardinals in the 1934 World Series, and awed fans and batters with his array of arm angles and sheer stuff. Rickey once was heard to remark, "I was in the top 10 percent of my law school class. I am a Doctor of Juris Prudence. I have an honorary Doctor of Laws. So, would somebody please tell me why I spent four mortal hours today conversing with a person named Dizzy Dean?" That stuff was the answer; it excused a lot.

MORT COOPER, RHP (1938–1945)

Fortunate enough not to be called into service in World War II, Cooper put a hurt on the thinned-out National League. From 1942-44, he went 65-22 with a 2.17 ERA, winning an MVP award and two World Series rings. Harry Brecheen was the lefty with the screwball; Cooper was the righty with one. The screwball works its titular magic on the arm eventually, so Cooper's career evaporated not long after the war, the wear exacerbated by a problematic off-field lifestyle that included too much drinking and other issues.

MAX LANIER, LHP (1938–1946, 1949–1951)
In the postwar period, Jorge Pasquel almost stole big-league baseball from the United States. He was never going to successfully dismantle the major leagues, but he came close to putting a huge dent in it by brazenly recruiting notable big-leaguers to sign for more money in the Mexican League. One of the few who took the plunge was Lanier, an early pioneer in the fight for ballplayers to be paid what they were worth rather than what owners decided they could spare. A lefty, Lanier used to pitch sidearm against lefties, then come right over the top with a high-spin heater against righties. He navigated elbow trouble his whole career, and some legal trouble after going to Mexico for two years, but had a long, impressive career.

HARRY BRECHEEN, LHP (1940, 1943–1952)
A little lefty without a big fastball, Harry the Cat kept hitters off-balance and off the bases. He had both a curveball and a screwball and could pair the two to great effect—something akin to the modern sinker-cutter artists, like Roy Halladay, but at half-speed. He didn't establish himself in the big leagues until he was 28, but once he did he posted a sub-3.00 career ERA in almost 2,000 innings. His 1946 World Series (complete-game wins in Games 2 and 6, the win in relief via getting the last six outs of Game 7) is one of the best any player ever had.

HOWIE POLLET, LHP (1941–1943, 1946–1951)
Sandwiching two years away in the Air Force (mostly playing ball, just in a different uniform), Pollet won ERA titles in 1943 and 1946. In the latter season, he also led the National League in innings pitched. With a windmill windup and a funky over-the-top left-handed delivery, he started losing zip on his fastball almost immediately after 1946 but hung around as an uneven but durable starter for another decade.

LARRY JACKSON, RHP (1955–1962)
Jackson came into the big leagues with a solid fastball-curveball mix but rose to stardom for the meat of his career because he got firmer command of his changeup and learned the slider. He paced the majors with 282 innings pitched in 1960 and was a steadily above-average starter for the Cardinals for a total of six seasons. Over that span, in addition to starting 30 games a year, he was called upon in relief 39 times. The 1962 trade that sent Jackson and Lindy McDaniel to the Cubs in return for George Altman, Moe Thacker, and Don Cardwell was one of the worst in team history, although it was somewhat ameliorated a month later when the Cardinals dealt Cardwell to the Pirates for shortstop Dick Groat.

BOB GIBSON, RHP (1959–1975)

For most of baseball history, the batter's fear of the pitched ball was an inextricable, even fundamental part of the game. It gave physical and psychological boundaries to the battle between batter and pitcher and allowed each encounter to act as a renegotiation of those boundaries. Gibson became a master of that chess game. He was no beanball artist but used the inside pitch to set up the one away. He paired a blazing fastball with a vicious power slider, all out of a near-flying delivery, and his mental domination of every at-bat sealed the deal. It's impossible to separate his legendary intensity from the extent to which the Cardinals, and manager Solly Hemus in particular, seemed indifferent to him at best. They made sure he always had something to prove, and for the worst reasons possible.

CHRIS CARPENTER, RHP (2004–2012)

His body tried hard to rebel against his relentless pitching, and force him to stop. Carpenter dealt with more than one serious injury, to his elbow and his shoulder. The Cardinals were able to scoop him up as a reclamation project after he missed all of 2003, but with Dave Duncan at his side, Carpenter crafted the most effective sinker of its era. He still lost most of 2007 and 2008, but won the 2005 Cy Young Award, the 2009 ERA title, and—his defining moment—five of six starts in the miraculous 2011 run that brought St. Louis its latest World Series.

ADAM WAINWRIGHT, RHP (2005–Present)

Everything with Wainwright is the arc of his curveball. His Twitter handle is @UncleCharlie50. The pitch that made him a St. Louis legend in October of his rookie season is still helping him, now in defiance of a traditional aging curve. The pitch is Wainwright's sextant and his rudder. He uses it to find his bearings when none of his other stuff is working, and then he uses it to get moving and escape trouble. Seasons lost to injury have pockmarked his career, but it's been a great one. Traded to the Cardinals by the Braves for one season of J.D. Drew and Eli Marrero 17 years ago and counting.

A Taxonomy of 2020 Abnormalities

by Rob Mains

I'm going to start this with a trivia question. Trust me, it's relevant. Don't bother skipping to the end of the article to find the answer, it's not there.

Only five players have appeared in 140 or more games for 16 straight seasons. Who are they?

It's a trivia question starting off an essay, so you know how this works: Whatever you guessed, you're wrong. It's okay. As someone who purchased this book, chances are good that you're an educated baseball fan. But the circumstances behind 2020 force us to abandon, or at least seriously question, some of our favorite patterns and crutches for evaluating the game we love.

We just completed what was undoubtedly the strangest season in MLB history. No fans, geographically limited schedule, universal DH, seven-inning twin bills, runners on second in extra innings, a 16-team postseason, a club playing at a Triple-A stadium. Some of these changes will likely persist (sorry), but we've never had so many tweaks dumped on us all at once, at least not since they figured out how many balls were in a walk.

And the biggest, of course, was the 60-game season. The 19th century was dotted with teams that went bankrupt before the season ended, but the lone season with only 60 scheduled games was 1877. That year there were only six teams, the league rostered a total of 77 players (just 16 more than the 2020 Marlins), and batters called for pitches to be thrown high or low by the pitcher, who was 50 feet away. We can say the 2020 season was easily the shortest ever for recognizable baseball.

As such, it'll stand out. Few abbreviated seasons do. Just about everybody reading this knows the 1994 season ended after Seattle's Randy Johnson struck out Oakland's Ernie Young for the last out of the Mariners-A's game on August 11. The ensuing player strike wiped out the rest of the season and the postseason. Teams played only 112-117 games that year.

And many of you know that a strike in the middle of the 1981 season split the season in two, resulting in the only Division Series until 1995. Teams played only 103-111 games that year, the shortest regular season since 1885.

Those two seasons are memorable. So when we see that nobody drove in 100 runs in 1981, or that Greg Maddux was the only pitcher with 180 or more innings pitched in 1994, we think, "Of course. Strike year."

But we don't remember other short years. You might not recall that the 1994 strike spilled into the next year, chopping 18 games off the 1995 schedule. You might've read that the 1918 season, played during the last pandemic, ended after Labor Day due to the government's World War I "work or fight" order. A strike erased the first week and a half of the 1972 season, but that year's best known as the last time pitchers batted in the American League.

The point is, while we don't remember small changes to the schedule, we remember the big ones. The 1981 mid-season strike. The 1994 season- and Series-ending strike. And, of course, the pandemic-shortened 2020 season. We won't need a reminder why Marcell Ozuna's 18 homers were the fewest to lead the National League in a century. (Literally; Cy Williams led with 15 in 1920.)

Now, about that trivia question. The five players are Hank Aaron, Brooks Robinson, Pete Rose, Ichiro Suzuki, and Johnny Damon. The one nobody gets, of course, is Damon, and a lot of people miss Ichiro, whose last season of 140-plus games came garbed in the red-orange and ocean blue of Miami when he was 42. That's half of what makes it a good question. The other half is the two guys whom many think made the list but didn't. Lou Gehrig? His streak started in the Yankees' 42nd game of the 1925 season and lasted only 13 seasons after that. And everybody assumes Cal Ripken Jr. did it, having played 2,632 straight games over 17 seasons. But one of those 17 seasons was 1994, when the Orioles played only 112 games.

My point? *I just told you* everybody remembers the 1994 strike year, but everybody forgets it fell in the middle of Ripken's streak, separating the first twelve years from the last four. Just because we recall something doesn't mean it's always at the front of our minds.

Nobody is going to forget 2020, and baseball is obviously not the main reason. But there will come a time in the future when you're looking at a player's or a team's record, and there will be baffling numbers there for 2020, and you'll think, "I wonder what happened." (Not to mention the missing line for minor league players.) Just like you forgot that the 1994 strike limited Ripken to 112 games.

Try not to forget it, though. The 2020 season resulted in weird statistical results for several reasons.

There were only 60 games.

I know, duh. But that had impacts beyond counting stats like Ozuna's home run total or Yu Darvish and Shane Bieber leading the majors with eight wins. (I know, pitcher wins, but still.)

The 162-game season is the longest among major North American sports, and that duration gives us a gift. Over the course of a long season, small variations tend to even out. A player who has a ten-game hot streak will probably have a ten-game cold streak. A team that starts the year losing a bunch of close games will probably win a bunch of them. We get regression to the mean. Statistics stabilize.

Consider flipping a coin. Over the long run, we expect it to come up heads about half the time. But the fewer flips, the more variation there'll be. If you flip a coin six times, probability theory tells us you'll get at least two-third heads about 34 percent of the time. Flip it 30 times, your chance of two-thirds heads drops to five percent.

Or, relevant to this case, if you flip a coin 60 times, your chance of getting at least 36 heads—that's 60 percent—is 7.75 percent. Expand the coin-flipping to 162 times, and the chance of getting 60 percent heads drops to 0.73 percent.

In other words, the odds of an outcome that's 20 percent better (or worse) than expected is *more than ten times higher* when you flip your coin 60 times than when you do it 162 times. Call it small sample size, call lack of mean reversion, or call it luck not evening out, 162 is a lot more predictive than 60. You get much more variation over 60 games than over 162. Bieber's 1.63 ERA and 0.87 FIP aren't something we'd see over a full season, and neither is Javier Baéz's .203/.238/.360.

Some players' lines in 2020 look normal. Brian Anderson had an .811 OPS in 2019 and an .810 OPS in 2020. (He probably would have gotten that last point if he'd been given enough time.) But there are many like Bieber and Baéz, some of them from young players still establishing their talent levels. The answer to the question, "What went right or wrong for that guy in 2020?" is most likely "Nothing, it was just a 2020 thing."

Preseason training was abbreviated for hitters.

Every year, spring training drags. Players get tired of it, fans get tired of it, and you sure can tell sportswriters get tired of it. Yes, something to get everyone into shape is necessary, but does it really have to drag on for over a month? Can't we shorten it?

The 2020 season answered in the negative, at least for hitters. Warren Spahn is credited with saying that hitting is timing and pitching is upsetting timing. It appears nobody had his timing down after the abbreviated July summer camp. Through August 9—18 games into the season—MLB batters were hitting .230/.311/.395 with a .275 BABIP. That BABIP, had it held, would have been the lowest since 1968, the Year of the Pitcher. In recent years it's hovered around .300.

It didn't hold. Play returned to more normal levels the rest of the year: .249/.325/.425 with a .297 BABIP starting August 10. But batters whose play concentrated in those first two weeks wound up with ugly lines. Andrew

Benintendi went on the injured list with a season-ending rib cage strain on August 11. His final line: .103/.314/.128 in 14 games. Franchy Cordero went on the IL with a hamate bone fracture on August 9 and a .154/.185/.231 line. Even though he came back strong in a late September return, it was too late to repair his full-season numbers.

Preseason training was abbreviated for pitchers.

Every year, spring training drags. Players get tired of it, fans get tired of it … wait, I already said that. But the abbreviated preseason was tough on pitchers, too. As noted, they had the upper hand coming out of the gate. But then they lost that hand. And then their arms, too.

The 2020 season was spread over 67 days. During those 67 days, 237 pitchers hit the Injured List, compared to 135 in the first 67 days of 2019. A lot of those IL stints, though, were COVID-19-related. Still, over the first 67 days of the 2019 season, there were 72 pitchers on the IL with arm injuries. That figure jumped to 110 in 2020, a 53 percent increase.

There are a number of factors contributing to pitcher arm injuries, ranging from usage to velocity, but it appears that attenuated preseason training played a role. A lot of pitchers had super-short seasons due to arm woes. Corey Kluber, Roberto Osuna, and Shohei Ohtani combined for seven innings, none after August 8. All suffered arm injuries. We'll never know whether they'd have fared better with a longer preseason, but we can guess how they probably feel.

Everybody played.

Rosters were set to expand from 25 to 26 in 2020, so even if we'd had a normal season, we'd have likely seen 2019's record of 1,410 players on MLB rosters broken. But due to the pandemic, rosters started the year at 30 and were cut to only 28. Add multiple COVID-19 absences and the revolving door caused by poor starts by hitters and a rash of pitcher arm injuries, and 1,289 players appeared in MLB games in 2020. The comparable figure over the first 67 days of the 2019 season was 1,109. That 16 percent increase works out to an average of six more players per team in 2020 compared to a similar slice of 2019. A future look back at 2020 rosters will include a lot of unfamiliar names.

Plus became a minus.

In advanced metrics, we adjust batter and pitcher performance for park and league/era variations. A plus sign appended to the end of a measure means that it's adjusted for park and league. It's scaled to an average of 100, with higher figures above average and lower figures below average. (Similarly, a metric with a minus is also park- and league-adjusted and scaled to 100, with lower values better.) Here at BP, our advanced measure of offensive performance is DRC+. Baseball-Reference has OPS+ and FanGraphs has wRC+.

Using park and league adjustments, we can compare Dante Bichette's 1995 Steroid Era season at pre-humidor Coors Field (.340/.364/.620, 40 homers, 128 RBI, MVP runner-up) with Jim Wynn's 1968 Year of the Pitcher season at the cavernous Astrodome (.269/.376/.474, 26 homers, 67 RBI, no MVP votes). It's not close. DRC+, OPS+, and wRC+ all give the nod to Wynn, handily. This is a useful tool. As my Baseball Prospectus colleague Patrick Dubuque tweeted last fall, "Please note that when I ask how you are, I am already adjusting for era."

The 2020 season messes up plus (and minus) stats for two reasons. First, the park adjustment was based on only 30 home games instead of the usual 81. Everything noted above regarding the short season applies, literally doubly, to park effect calculations. DRC+ uses a single-season park factor. OPS+ uses a three-year average and wRC+ five years. The figure for 2020 is suspect.

Second, OPS+ and wRC+ adjust for league: American and National. (DRC+ adjusts for opponent, regardless of league.) While there were two leagues in 2020, they were an artificial construct. To reduce travel, teams played opponents geographically, not based on league. There weren't two leagues, American and National. There were three, Western, Central, and Eastern.

That makes a difference because teams in the same league played in different run-scoring environments. AL teams scored 4.58 runs per game, NL teams 4.71. That's a small difference. But teams in the East scored 0.21 more runs per game (4.95) than teams in the West (4.74), and they both scored a lot more than Central teams (4.25). Adjusting for league misses that difference, so this book will be safe in that regard, but other sources may be distorted somewhat.

Not every game was a "game."
In 2020, the rising tide of strikeouts was finally stemmed. Strikeouts per team per game fell from 8.8 in 2019 to 8.7 in 2020. That marked the first decline after 14 straight annual increases.

In 2020, the rising tide of strikeouts rose higher. Batters struck out in 23.4 percent of plate appearances compared to 23.0 percent in 2019. That marked the 15th straight annual increase.

Both are true statements.

Because of two rule changes—seven-inning doubleheaders and runners on second in extra innings—games in 2020 were unprecedented in their brevity. There were 37.0 plate appearances per game in 2020. The only years with fewer were 1904 and 1906-1909. The average game in 2020 entailed 8.61 innings pitched, the fewest since 1899.

So when you see any per-game stats for 2020, you need to increase them by 3 or 4 percent to get them on equal footing with recent years.

St. Louis Cardinals 2021

Or, better, just ignore them. Last year happened. There were major league games contested between major league teams. But when you're looking at those physical or electronic baseball cards, when you're weaving narratives over why this young player's inevitable rise to stardom fell apart or why that old veteran rekindled his magic, don't linger on the 2020 line. It was just too weird.

Thanks to Lucas Apostoleris for research assistance.

—*Rob Mains is an author of Baseball Prospectus.*

Tranches of WAR

by Russell A. Carleton

We ask "replacement level" to be a lot of things. Sometimes contradictory things. Sometimes I wonder if we know what it even means anymore. The original idea was that it represented the level of production that a team could expect to get from "freely available talent", including bench players, minor leaguers, and waiver wire pickups. It created a common benchmark to compare everyone to, and for that reason, it represented an advancement well beyond what was available at the time. In fact, it created a language and a framework for evaluating players that was not just better but *entirely* different than what came before it.

But then we started mumbling in that language. The idea behind "wins above replacement" was one part sci-fi episode and one part mathematical exercise. Imagine that a player had disappeared before the season and suddenly, in an alternate timeline, his team would have had to replace him. The distance between him and that replacement line was his value. We need to talk about that alternate timeline.

Without getting too into 2:00 am "deep conversations" with extensive navel-gazing, it's worth thinking about why one player might not be playing, while another might.

- A player might not be playing because he has a short-term injury or his manager believes that he needs a day off.
- A player might not be playing because he has a longer-term injury that requires him to be on the injured list.

There's a difference here between these two situations. In particular, the first one generally *doesn't* involve a compensatory roster move, while the second one does. It's possible, though not guaranteed, that the person who will be replacing the injured/resting player would be the same in either case. That matters. Teams generally carry a spare part for all eight position players on the diamond, although in the era of a four-player bench, those spare parts usually are the backup plan for more than one spot.

St. Louis Cardinals 2021

A couple of years ago, I posed a hypothetical question. Suppose that a team had two players in its system fighting for a fourth outfielder spot. One of them was a league average hitter, but would be worth 20 runs below average if allowed to play center field for a full season. One of them was a perfectly average fielder, but would be 15 runs below average as a hitter, if allowed to play an entire season. Which of the two should the team roster? It's tempting to say the second one, as overall, he is the better player. That misses the point. A league average hitter on the bench isn't just a potential replacement for an injured outfielder. He might also pinch hit for the light-hitting shortstop in a key spot. You keep the average hitter on the roster, even though he isn't a hand-in-glove fit for one specific place on the field, because being a bench player is a different job description than being a long-term fill-in for someone. If you find yourself in need of a longer-term fill-in, you can bring the other guy up from AAA.

When we're determining the value of an everyday player though, if he had disappeared before the season and a team would have had to replace his production, they likely would have done it with a player who was a long-term fill-in type because they would have had to replace a guy who played everyday. Maybe that's the same guy that they would have rostered on their bench anyway, but we don't know. It gets to the query of what we hope to accomplish with WAR. Are we looking for an accurate modeling of reality or are we looking for a common baseline to compare everyone to? Both have their uses, but they are somewhat different questions.

Let's talk about another dichotomy.

- A player might not be playing because he isn't very good and is a bench-level player.
- A player might not be playing because there is another player on the team who has a situational advantage that makes him the better choice today. The classic case of this is a handedness platoon. On another day, he might be a better choice.

When we think about player usage, I think we're still stuck in the model that there are starters and there are scrubs. We have plenty of words for bench players or reserves or backups or utility guys. We do still have the word "platoon" in our collective vocabulary, but in the age of short benches, it's hard to construct one. It's always been hard to construct them. You have to find two players who hit with different hands, have skill sets that complement each other, and probably play the same position. In the era of the short bench, one of them had probably better double as a utility player in some way. Baseball has a two-tiered language geared toward the idea of regulars and reserves. The fact that it was so easy for me to find plenty of synonyms for "a player whose primary function is to come into a game to replace a regular player if he is injured or resting" should tell you something.

I'm always one to look for "unspoken words" in baseball. What is it called when someone is both half of a platoon and the utility infielder? That guy exists sometimes, but he reveals himself in that role—usually by accident. We don't have a word for that, and whenever I find myself saying "we don't have a word for that", I look for new opportunities. What do you call it, further, when the job of being the utility infielder is decentralized across the whole infield with occasional contributions from the left fielder? It's not even a "super-utility" player. What happens when you build your entire roster around the idea that everyone will be expected to be a triple major?

⚾ ⚾ ⚾

I think someone else beat me to this one, and on a grand scale. Platoons work because we know that hitters of the opposite hand to the pitcher get better results than hitters of the same hand, usually to the tune of about 20 points of OBP. If you want to express that in runs, it usually comes out to somewhere around 10 to 12 runs of linear weights value prorated across 650 PA. But hang on a second, now let's say that we have two players who might start today, both of roughly equal merit with the bat. One has a handedness advantage, but is the worse fielder of the two. In that case, as long as his "over the course of a season" projection as a fielder at whatever position you want to slot him into is less than a 10-run drop from the guy he might replace, then he's a better option today.

We're not used to thinking of utility players as bat-first options, who would play below-average defense at three different infield positions. That guy might hook on as a 2B/3B/LF type (Howie Kendrick, come on down!) but teams usually think to themselves that they need as their utility infielder someone who "can handle" shortstop, the toughest of the infield spots to play. If someone can do that *and* hit well, he's probably already starting somewhere, so he's not available as a utility infielder. It's easier for those glove guys to find a job. In a world where the replacement for a shortstop *has to be* the designated utility infielder, that makes sense.

But as we talked about last week, we're living in a different world. The rate at which a replacement for a regular starter turns out to be *another starter* shifting over to cover has gone way up over the last five years. There was always some of it in the game, but this has been a supernova of switcheroos. Now if your second baseman is capable of playing a decent shortstop, that 2B/3B/LF guy can swap in. He's not actually playing shortstop, and maybe the defense suffers from the switch, but if he's got enough of a bat, he might outhit those extra fielding miscues. And in doing so, he is effectively your backup shortstop.

Somewhere along the lines, teams got hip to the idea of multi-positional play from their regulars. I've written before about how you can't just put a player, however athletic, into a new position and expect much at first. The data tell us that. Eventually, players can learn to be multi-positionalists, but it takes time, roughly on the order of two months, before they're OK. But there's a hidden message in there. If you give a player some reps at a new spot, he's a reasonably gifted athlete and somewhat smart and willing to learn, he could probably pick it up enough to get to "good enough," and it doesn't take forever. You just have to be purposeful about it. Maybe you get to the point where you can start to say "he's still below average but we could move him there and get another bat into the lineup, and it's a net win."

Teams have started to build those extra lessons into their player development program. It used to be seen as a mark of weakness to be relegated to "utility player" because that meant that you were a bench player (all those synonyms above come with a side of stigma). Now, it's a way of building a team. If you get a few reps in the minors (where it doesn't count) at a spot, you'll have at least played the spot at game speed before. There are limits to how far you can push that. A slow-footed "he's out in left field because we don't have the DH" guy is never going to play short, but maybe your third baseman can try second base and not look like a total moose out there.

⚾ ⚾ ⚾

Back to WAR. I'd argue that the world of starters and scrubs is slowly disintegrating, for good cause. In the event that a regular starter really does go down with an injury–ostensibly, the alternate universe scenario that WAR is attempting to model–it makes the team a little more resilient to replacing him. And the good news is that you're more likely to be able to replace him with the best of the bench bunch, rather than the third-best guy, because the best guy doesn't have to be an exact positional match for the guy who got hurt. And that's what the manager would want to do. He'd want to replace that long-term production, not with an amalgam of everyone else who played that position, but with the best guy available from his reserves.

Now this is still WAR. We still want to retain the principle that we should be measuring a player, and not his teammates. We need some sort of common baseline, and despite what I just said, we'll still need some sort of amalgam. To construct that, I give to you the idea of the tranche. The word, if you've not heard it before, refers to a piece of a whole that is somehow segmented off. It's often used in finance to talk about layers of a financial instrument.

Here, I want you to consider that there are 30 starters at each of the seven non-battery positions (catchers should have their own WAR, since only a catcher can replace a catcher). We can identify them by playing time, and we can futz around with the definition a little bit if we need to. Next, among those who aren't in that starting pool, we identify the top tranche of the 30 best bench players, which I would again identify by playing time, and then the second and third and fourth and so on. If a player were to disappear, his manager would probably want to take a guy from that top tranche of the bench to replace him. In a world where even the starters can slide around the field, that becomes more feasible.

We can take a look at that top tranche and say "How many of them showed that they are able to play (first, second, etc.)?" and therefore could have directly substituted for the starter? How many of them could have been a direct substitute for our injured player? We don't know whether one of them would be on *a specific* team, but we can say that 40 percent of the time, a manager would have been able to draw from tranche 1 in filling the role, and 35 percent from tranche 2. But on tranche 1, we can also look at how many of those players played a position that could have then shifted and covered for that spot. We'd need some eligibility criteria for all of this (probably a minimum number of games played) but it would just be a matter of multiplication. Shortstop would be harder to fill, and managers would probably be dipping a little further down in the talent pool, and so replacement level would be lower, as it is now.

Doing some quick analysis, I found that the difference in just batting linear weights (haven't even gotten into running or fielding) between tranche 1 and tranche 2 in 2019 was about 6.5 runs, prorated across 650 PA. Between tranche 1 and tranche 3, it's 10.8 runs. The ability to shift those plate appearances up the ladder has some real value.

This part is important. We can also give credit to starters for the positions that they showed an ability to play, even if they didn't play them (this is the guy fully capable of playing center, but who's in a corner because the team already has a good center fielder) because he allows a team to carry a player who hits like a left fielder to functionally be the team's backup center fielder. He facilitates that movement upward among the tranches. We can start to appreciate the difference between a left fielder who would never be able to hack it in center (and the compensatory move that his team would have to make) and the left fielder who could do it, but just didn't have to very often.

Past that, you can continue to use whatever hitting and fielding and running metrics you like to determine a player's value, but when we get down to constructing that baseline, I'd argue we need a better conceptual and mathematical framework. It's going to require some more #GoryMath than we're used to, but I'd argue it's a better conceptualization of the way that MLB actually plays the game in 2020. If…y'know…MLB plays in 2020. If WAR is going to be our flagship statistic among the *acronymati*, then we need to acknowledge that it contains some old and starting-to-be-out-of-date assumptions about the game. We may need to tinker with it. Here's my idea for how.

—*Russell A. Carleton is an author of Baseball Prospectus.*

Secondhand Sport

by Patrick Dubuque

Back before time stopped, I liked to go to thrift stores. Now that I'm older, I rarely ever buy anything—I don't need much in my life, now—but I still enjoy the old familiar circuit: check to see if there are baseball cards to write about, look for board or card games to play with the kids, scan for random ironic jerseys, hit the book section. It takes ten, maybe fifteen minutes. Thrift stores are the antithesis of modern online shopping, because you don't know what they have, and you don't even really know what you want. It's junk, literal junk, stuff other people thought was worthless. That's what makes it great.

In an idealized economy, thrift stores shouldn't exist. Everybody has a living wage, and every product has a durability that exactly matches its desired life; nothing should need to be given away, no one should need to be given to. But then, thrift stores shouldn't work on a customer experience level, either. You wouldn't think an ethos of "let's make everything disorganized and hard to find" would lead to customer satisfaction, but low-budget retailers like TJ Maxx and Ross thrive on this model. People like bargain hunting as much for the hunting as the bargain; it's part of the experience, spending time as if it's a wager. There's a thrill, occasionally, in inefficiency.

In sports, the modern overuse of the word "inefficiency" is a condemnation: It insinuates that there is *an* efficiency, a correct way to be found, and that all other ways are wrong ways. It's prevalent in baseball but hardly contained to it; the lifehack, the Silicon Valley disruption are other examples of productivity creep in our daily lives. Their modern success makes plenty of sense. Maximization of resources, after all, is its own puzzle, and an industry of European board games is founded upon it. It's fun to take a system and optimize it, unravel it like a sudoku puzzle. If there's only one kind of genius, after all, there's no way anyone can fail to appreciate it.

Baseball has been hacking away at these perceived inefficiencies since its inception: platoons, bullpens, farm systems were all installed to extract more out of the tools at hand. But it's been a particular badge of the sabermetric movement, from Ken Phelps and his All-Star Team to Ricardo Rincon and the darlings of *Moneyball*. It's business, but it's also an ethos: the idea that there's treasure among the trash, something we all failed to appreciate until someone brought it to light.

It's the myth that made Sidd Finch so enticing, that fuels so many "best shape" narratives and new pitch promises. We all, athletes and unathletic sportswriters, want to believe that there's genius trapped inside us, and that it's just a matter of puzzling out the combination to unlock it. That our art, our style is the next inefficiency, waiting for our own Billy Beane. It's why we root for underdogs, and why we're excited for the Mike Tauchmans and the Eurubiel Durazos, champions of skin-deep mediocrity.

Except we aren't anymore, really. The days of "Free X" have descended beyond the ring of irony and into obscurity. There are still Xs to be freed, or at least one X, duplicated endlessly: Mike Ford, Luke Voit, Max Muncy. The undervalued one-dimensional slugger demonstrated how the game hasn't quite culturally caught up to its logical extreme. But for those who don't fit the rather spacious mold, times are grimmer. As Rob Arthur revealed several months ago, there's been a marked increase in the number of sub-replacement relievers. It's the outcome of a greater number of teams forced to play out games without the talent to win them, but it's also emblematic of the modern tendency of teams to dispose of their disposable assets, burning through cost-controlled arms the way that man chopped down forests in *The Lorax*. Stuff just isn't built to outlive their original owners anymore.

It's unsurprising, given how well-mined the market for inefficiencies has been of late. The disciples of the early analytics departments, and the disciples of those, have proliferated the league, with only a few backwater holdouts. The league has grown smarter, but every team has learned the same lesson. In fact, the phenomenon creates a peculiar kind of feedback loop: As teams value a specific subset of players or skills, prospective athletes learn to increase their own marketability by conforming themselves to the demands of their prospective employers.

And that's tragic, in the way that the extinction of animals is tragic; a certain amount of biodiversity in baseball has been lost. Shortstops hit like outfielders. Pitchers don't hit at all. Only the catchers remain idiosyncratic, thanks to the defensive demands of their position; eventually they too will be required to produce like everyone else, or they'll meet the fate of their battery mates. A perfect economy requires perfect production.

I mentioned earlier that more and more, I leave thrift stores empty-handed. It is true that I am more discerning than in the past; my bookshelves are full, and there are more streaming films than I will ever be able to watch. But there are other factors at play.

Thrift stores are, in a way, the bond markets of retail. When the economy is rough and other retailers are struggling, more people look secondhand for their products. But as recently as last year, publications were noting a reversal of the trend: Companies like Goodwill and Savers were expanding despite a strong economy. Publications credited a heightened sense of environmentalism and a rejection of cutting-edge fashion as drivers behind the increase, though the more likely answer is the modern American economy hasn't showered its favors equally, particularly among the young.

But it is more than just the economy. Baseball and thrift stores share something else in common, evident in our current conversations about re-starting the sport: They live in the gray area between public service and private enterprise. Thrift stores provide affordable necessities to lower-class citizens, and collectibles and fashion for the middle-class. Because of the success of the latter, prices have gone up across the board. Especially in terms of clothing, the middle-class flight from fashion into vintage has instead carried the aftereffects of fashion, including its costs, into a territory where people just want clothes. But there's another factor in the rise of prices, in the form of the internet.

The Goodwills of the world have grown smarter, too, employing the internet to extract full value from their detritus. Ebay, similarly, has lost much of the charm it had as a new frontier around the turn of the century. Everything has a price point now; even individual taste is no match for the algorithm, because anything rare, no matter how niche its market, is a collectible to someone.

The internet has had the same effect on thrift stores that sabermetrics has had on baseball; its equivalent to OBP was the bar scanner. As detailed in Slate, the rise of second-party stores on eBay and Amazon birthed an entire industry of used-good salespeople, armed with PDAs and scanners, buying books for three dollars to sell online for five. The author, Michael Savitz, reports earning $60,000 by working nearly 80 hours a week; he makes it clear that this is not a vocation of his choosing. It's long hours, with no real creativity or individuality, skimming the cream off of a local establishment and flipping it to someone with a little more money on the other side of the country. And once the vocation exists, the obvious question arises: why wait to put the wares out on the shelves? Why allow value to exist at all?

Nothing is ruined. Thrift stores will continue to sell polo shirts and DVDs, and baseball will continue to exist and make or lose money, depending on who you believe. But as we continue to refine our knowledge, we lose something in the conquest for efficiency, a delight born out of the unknown. The problem isn't the efficiency itself; we can't blame the booksellers, or the people sweeping freeways to collect grams of platinum from damaged catalytic converters. The problem is a system that requires this sort of profit-skimming behavior in order to feed families (or, for corporations, maximize shareholder return).

St. Louis Cardinals 2021

In times like these, with the 2020 season on the brink and the collective bargaining agreement close behind, it can often feel like the current situation is untenable. It can't keep going like this, even if we don't know what to do about it. But as with thrift stores, there's an equally irresistible feeling that it *has* to keep going, that it would be unimaginable to not have this broken, amazing sport. Both industries exist on an invisible foundation of friction, of chaos and unpredictability, even as both see their foundations buffed down to a perfect, untouchable polish. But if COVID-19 and its financial ramifications do, as some have suggested, make it such that the baseball that returns is fundamentally different than the baseball that came before, perhaps this is the time to lean in, and change the game even more. Fix bunting. Make defense more difficult. Create viable, alternate strategies. Add some chaos back into baseball. It's fun when no one knows quite where things are.

—Patrick Dubuque is an author of Baseball Prospectus.

Steve Dalkowski Dreaming

by Steven Goldman

We dream of being a pitcher, of starring in the major leagues. Depending on your age and your sense of historical perspective, you might imagine yourself as Walter Johnson, throwing harder than anyone else—hitting more batters than anyone else, too, but always feeling bad about it. You could picture yourself as a Tom Seaver or a David Cone, with all the stuff in the world but still being cerebral about it, thinking about so much more than burning 'em in there. There are so many models one could choose: You could be a Lefty Gomez, Jim Bouton, or Bill Lee, skilled, but not taking the whole thing too seriously, or a Lefty Grove, Bob Gibson, or Steve Carlton, powerful but treating each start like a mission to be survived instead of a game to be enjoyed.

Very few would dream of being Steve Dalkowski, the former Baltimore Orioles prospect who died of COVID-19 last week at the age of 80. Yet, there is something just as noble in Dalkowski's negative accomplishments—and accomplishments is what they are—as there is in the precision-engineered pitching of a Greg Maddux. You have to be very good to be that bad. Dalkowski had all of the stuff of the greatest pitchers but none of the command; his story is not one of failing to conquer his limitations, but striving against one of the cruelest hands that fate or genetics or personality can deal us: A desire to achieve great things which is almost but not quite matched by the ability to meet that goal.

As with Johnson, Grove, Bob Feller, and the rest of the hard-throwing pitchers who played before the advent of modern radar guns, we have to take the word of the players and coaches who saw Dalkowski pitch as to his velocity. He was a hard-drinking, maximum-effort pitcher who, if their memories are to be believed, consistently threw over 100 miles per hour. His was the Maltese Fastball, the stuff that dreams are made of. The problem is that velocity without command and control is still a good distance from utility. Dalkowski was the most effective towel you could design for a fish, the sleekest bathing suit intended to be worn by an astronaut, but that doesn't mean he wasn't beautiful: We can appreciate a journey even if it doesn't end at the intended destination.

Whether because of sloppy mechanics he couldn't calm, an inability to understand that a consistent 98 in the strike zone would likely be more effective than a consistent 110 out of it, or all that beer, Dalkowski could never make the adjustments that pitchers like Feller and Nolan Ryan made before him, possibly because he had so far to go: Feller, who never pitched in the minors, came up at 17 and spent three years walking almost seven batters per nine innings before settling in at 3.8 beginning when he was 20. Ryan started out walking over six batters per nine but gradually improved as his long career played out; for him to go from 6.2 walks per nine with the 1966 Greenville Mets to 3.7 with the 1989 Texas Rangers represents a 40 percent reduction. An equivalent improvement by Dalkowski would still have left him walking over 11 batters per nine innings.

Dalkowski was like *The Room* of pitchers, a player so bad he became good again. Cal Ripken, Sr., who both played with and managed Dalkowski, recalled in a 1979 *Sporting News* "where are they now" piece the occasion when the pitcher crossed up his catcher and his fastball, "hit the plate umpire smack in the mask. The mask broke all to pieces and the umpire wound up in the hospital for three days with a concussion. If they ever had a radar gun in those days, I'll bet Dalkowski would have been timed at 110 miles an hour."

Signed by the Orioles out of New Britain High in Connecticut in 1957, Dalkowski was sent to Kingsport in the Appalachian League, where he pitched 62 innings. He allowed only 22 hits in 62 innings, or 3.2 per nine, a number with no equivalent in major league history (though Aroldis Chapman came close in 2014), and also struck out 121 (17.6 per nine) and walked 129 (18.7). He was also charged with 39 wild pitches. That June, one of his fastballs clipped a Dodgers prospect named Bob Beavers and carried away part of his ear. "The first pitch was over the backstop, the second pitch was called a strike, I didn't think it was," Beavers said last year. "The third pitch hit me and knocked me out, so I don't remember much after that. I couldn't get in the sun for a while, and I never did play baseball again." Former minor leaguer Ron Shelton based the *Bull Durham* pitcher Nuke LaLoosh on Dalkowski. And yet, to see him as a figure of fun, an amusing loser, is to misunderstand something unique and strange.

Dalkowski kept on posting some of the strangest lines in baseball history. Pitching for the Stockton Ports of the Class C California League in 1960, he struck out 262 and walked 262 in 170 innings. Yet, he did improve, especially after pitching for Earl Weaver at Elmira in 1962. Weaver had previously had Dalkowski at Aberdeen in 1959, but wasn't ready to grapple with him then. This time he was. "I had grown more and more concerned about players with great physical abilities who could not learn to correct certain basic deficiencies no matter how much you instructed or drilled them," he related in his autobiography, *It's What You Learn After You Know It All That Counts*. He got permission from the Orioles to give all of his players the Stanford-Binet IQ test. "Dalkowski finished in the 1 percentile in his ability to understand facts. Steve, it was said to say, had the ability to do everything but learn." [sic]

IQ tests are problematic diagnostic tools, so take Weaver's estimate of Dalkowski's mental capabilities with a grain of salt. What's important is that even if he got to the right answer by way of the wrong reason, Weaver had learned something valuable. His insight was to stop asking Dalkowski to learn new pitches and just let him get by with the two that he had. Were Dalkowski a prospect today, that would have been a no-brainer: Can't develop a third pitch? The bullpen is right over there, sir. Player development wasn't like that then, but Weaver, temporarily Dalkowski's mentor, could let him work with what he had. According to Weaver, the pitcher responded: "In the final 57 innings he pitched that season Dalkowski gave up 1 earned run, struck out 110 batters, and walked only 11." It's not true—as per the *Elmira Star-Gazette*, as of late July, Dalkowski had walked 71 in 106 innings and finished with 114 in 160 innings, which means Dalkowski's control actually faded at the end of the season rather than improved—but that doesn't mean it didn't happen in some sense, just that it didn't happen that way. Again, it's the journey, not the destination, and his ERA was 3.04 so *something* had gone right.

Also along the way: The next spring, Orioles manager Billy Hitchcock was rooting for Dalkowski to make the team as a long-man—maybe Weaver had gotten through to him. There were things out of Weaver's control, like the universe's twisted sense of humor: that March, Dalkowski's elbow went "twang."

You sometimes read that it was the Orioles' insistence on Dalkowski learning the curve that did him in, but even if they hadn't learned their lesson, the injury was probably just a coincidence: Dalkowski had thrown an incredible number of pitches over the previous few years. Still, it testifies to the dangers of trying to get what you want and risking the loss of what you had. Dalkowski tried to come back, but the 110-mph stuff was gone. A pitcher with no control and no stuff is…a civilian. What followed were years of vagabond living, arrests for drunkenness. There were Alcoholics Anonymous meetings, assistance from baseball alumni associations, but none of it took. From the 1990s until the time of his passing he dwelt in an assisted living facility, suffering from alcohol-related dementia. He'd been a heavy drinker since his teenage years. As with all those pitches per game, there was a price to be paid. You make choices on the journey and some of them are irrevocable. It's like a fairy tale: "Bite of poison apple? Don't mind if I do."

In the aforementioned *Sporting News* profile, Chuck Stevens, the head of the Association of Professional Ballplayers of America, a ballplayer charity, said, "I've got nothing against drinking. I do it myself sometimes. But, I don't condone common drunkenness. We went through lots of heartache and many dollars, but Dalkowski didn't want to help himself and we weren't going to keep him drunk." The journey is *un*like a fairy tale: No one will come along and kiss it better, not if they're busy forming judgments.

In the end, we are left with a sort of philosophical chicken/egg conundrum: Is failing to meet your goals evidence of unfulfilled potential or the lack of it? Isn't what you did by definition what you were capable of doing? Or could you have broken through to something better with the right help, the right lucky break? These are unanswerable questions, and how we try to answer them may say more about us than about the people we're judging.

No pitcher ever has it easy. *All* pitchers must work hard. *All* pitchers must refine their craft. It's almost never just about *stuff*. Dalkowski dreaming is no insult to the great pitchers who made it; from Pete Alexander to Max Scherzer, they have all earned their way up. And yet, if it is true that we can only do as much as we can do, then the journey would be more of an adventure, the ultimate triumph or defeat more noble, if like Dalkowski we lacked 100 percent of the confidence, the command, the self-possession, the commitment, the resistance to making bad decisions that so many great players possess—to be gloriously human. Or, to put it more succinctly, it would be fun to be able to throw as hard as any person ever has. Even if just for a moment, and even if nothing more came of it than that, no one could say you hadn't lived life to the fullest.

—*Steven Goldman is an author of Baseball Prospectus.*

A Reward For A Functioning Society

by Cory Frontin and Craig Goldstein

On July 5, Nationals reliever Sean Doolittle said in the middle of a press conference regarding the restart of Major League Baseball and what would later be known as summer camp, "sports are like the reward of a functioning society." This sentence was amidst a much longer, thoughtful reply about the societal and health conditions under which MLB players were being brought back. It's a very similar sentiment to one Jane McManus used on April 7, when she discussed the White House's meeting with sports commissioners. She said "sports are the effect of a functioning society—not the precursor."

Both versions of the same sentiment spoke to a laudable ideal in the context of a country that was not addressing a rampaging virus, and opting instead to bring sports back for the feeling of normalcy rather than the reality of it. "Priorities," as McManus said.

On Wednesday, the NBA's Milwaukee Bucks conducted a wildcat/political strike, refusing to come out for Game 5 of their playoff series against the Orlando Magic. The Magic refused to accept the forfeit, and shortly thereafter other playoff series were threatened by player strikes. Eventually the league moved to postpone that day's games, folding to players leveraging their united power.

The backdrop against which these actions took place was the shooting by police of Jacob Blake. Blake was shot in the back seven times by police, as he attempted to get into his vehicle. He managed to survive the assault, but is paralyzed from the waist down.

⚾   ⚾   ⚾

The step taken to walk out, first by the Milwaukee Bucks, then subsequently by other NBA, WNBA, and MLB teams, was a step toward upholding the virtue of the sentiment described by McManus and Doolittle. But that sentiment does not align with the broad history of sports in this and other countries, a history that contradicts the core of the idealistic statement.

Sports have been a significant part of American society for most of its existence, expanding in importance and influence in recent years. The idea that society was functioning in a way that was worthy of the reward of sports for most of that time is laughable. Much of America is not functioning and has not functioned for Black people, full stop. The oppressed people at the center of this political act by players, specifically Black players, in concert throughout the NBA and in fits and starts throughout Major League Baseball, have not known a society that functions for them rather than *because* of them.

Politics has been part of the sports landscape since the inception of sport, but for just about as long people have bemoaned its presence. Sports are to be an escape, it is said. An escape from what, though? A functioning society?

No, the presence of sports has never signified a cultural or political system that is on the up and up. Rather, the presence of sports *reflect and reinforce the society that produces them.*

⚾   ⚾   ⚾

The Negro Leagues were born out of societal dysfunction. The need for entirely separate leagues, composed of Black and Latino players barred from the Major Leagues because of racism? That is not a functioning society, and yet there were sports.

Even the integration of players from the Negro Leagues resulted in a transfer of power and wealth from Black-owned businesses and communities and into white ones, mirroring the dysfunction that had bled into every aspect of American society at the time. Japheth Knopp noted in the Spring 2016 Baseball Research Journal:

> *The manner in which integration in baseball—and in American businesses generally—occurred was not the only model which was possible. It was likely not even the best approach available, but rather served the needs of those in already privileged positions who were able to control not only the manner in which desegregation occurred, but the public perception of it as well in order to exploit the situation for financial gain. Indeed, the very word integration may not be the most applicable in this context because what actually transpired was not so much the fair and equitable combination of two subcultures into one equal and more homogenous group, but rather the reluctant allowance—under certain preconditions—for African Americans to be assimilated into white society.*

To understand the value of a movement, though, is not to understand how it is co-opted by ownership, but to know the people it brings together and what they demand. When Jackie Robinson—the player who demarcated the inevitability of the end of the Negro leagues—attended the March on Washington for Jobs and Freedom in 1963, he did so with his family and marched alongside the people. He stood alongside hundreds of thousands to fight for their common civil and labor rights. "The moral arc of the universe is long," many freedom fighters have echoed, "but it bends towards justice." The bend, it is less frequently said, happens when a great mass of people place the moral arc of the universe on their knee and apply force, as Jackie, his family, and thousands of others did that day.

⚾ ⚾ ⚾

Of course, taking the moral arc of the universe down from the mantle and bending it is not without risk. Perhaps the outsized influence of athletes is itself a mark of a dysfunctional society, but, nonetheless, hundreds of athletes woke up on Wednesday morning with the power to bring in millions of dollars in revenues. That very power, as we would come to find out, was matched with the equal and opposite power to *not* bring those revenues. That power, in hands ranging from the Milwaukee Bucks, to Kenny Smith in the *Inside the NBA* Studio, from the unexpected ally, Josh Hader, and his largely white teammates to the notably Black Seattle Mariners, would be exercised for a single demand: the end to state violence against Black people. Not unlike the March itself, it sat at the intersection of the civil rights of Black Americans and bold labor action. The March on Washington stood in the face of a false notion of integration—against an integration of extraction but not one of equality—and proposed something different. Just the same, the acts of solidarity of August 26, 2020 will be remembered in stark defiance of MLB's BLM-branded, but ultimately empty displays on opening weekend.

Bold defiance like this can never be without risk. By choosing to exercise this power, the Milwaukee Bucks took a risk. They risked vitriol and backlash from those they disagreed with. They risked fines or seeing their contracts voided, as a walkout like this is prohibited by their CBA. They risked forfeiting a playoff game, one that, as the No. 1 seed in the playoffs, they'd worked all year to attain. They didn't know how Orlando would respond. It wasn't clear that other teams throughout the league would follow suit in solidarity. And it wasn't known the league would accept these actions and moderately co-opt them by "postponing" games that would have featured no players.

If the league reschedules the games, some of the athletes' risk—their shared sacrifice—will be diminished, in retrospect. But they did not know any of that when they took that risk. And it is often left to athletes to take these risks when others in society won't, especially those of their same socioeconomic status and levels of influence.

It is athletes, specifically BIPOC athletes, that take them, though, because they live with the risk of being something other than white in this country every day. They are no strangers to the realities of police brutality. It seems incongruous then, to say that sports are a reward for a functioning society when we rely on athletes to lead us closer to being a functioning society. Luckily, our beloved athletes, WNBA players first and foremost among them, understand what sports truly are: a pipebender for the moral arc of the universe.

> —*Craig Goldstein is editor in chief of Baseball Prospectus. Cory Frontin is an author of Baseball Prospectus.*

Index of Names

Arenado, Nolan 16
Bader, Harrison 18
Bedell, Ian 90
Burleson, Alec 90
Cabrera, Génesis 34
Carlson, Dylan 20, 83
Carpenter, Matt 22
Dean, Austin 65
DeJong, Paul 24
Edman, Tommy 26
Elledge, Seth 36
Fernández, Junior 75
Flaherty, Jack 38
Gallegos, Giovanny 40
Gant, John 76
Goldschmidt, Paul 28
Gorman, Nolan 65, 84
Helsley, Ryan 42
Hence, Tink 76, 89
Herrera, Ivan 66, 87
Hicks, Jordan 77
Hudson, Dakota 44
Kaminsky, Rob 77
Kim, Kwang Hyun 46
Knizner, Andrew 67
Liberatore, Matthew 78, 85
Martínez, Carlos 48
Mendoza, Evan 91
Mikolas, Miles 79
Miller, Andrew 50
Miller, Brad 68
Molina, Yadier 30
Nogowski, John 69
Nunez, Edwin 90
O'Neill, Tyler 32
Oviedo, Johan 52, 87
Ponce de Leon, Daniel 54
Ramirez, Roel 80
Reyes, Alex 56
Sánchez, Ali 69
Sánchez, Ricardo 80
Sosa, Edmundo 70
Thomas, Lane 71
Thompson, Zack 81, 86
Torres, Jhon 71
Wainwright, Adam 59
Walker, Jordan 72, 85
Webb, Tyler 61
Whitley, Kodi 82, 89
Wieters, Matt 73
Williams, Justin 74
Winn, Masyn 74, 88
Woodford, Jake 63

For the Joy of Keeping Score

THIRTY81 Project is an ongoing graphic design project focused on the ballparks of baseball. Since being established in 2013, scorecards have been a fundemantal part of the effort. Each two-page card is uniquely ballpark-centric — there are 30 variants — and designed with both beginning and veteran scorekeepers in mind. Evolving over the years with suggestions from fans, broadcasters, and official scorers, the sheets are freely available to everyone as printable letter-size PDFs at the project webshop: www.THIRTY81Project.com

Download, Print, Score, Repeat ...

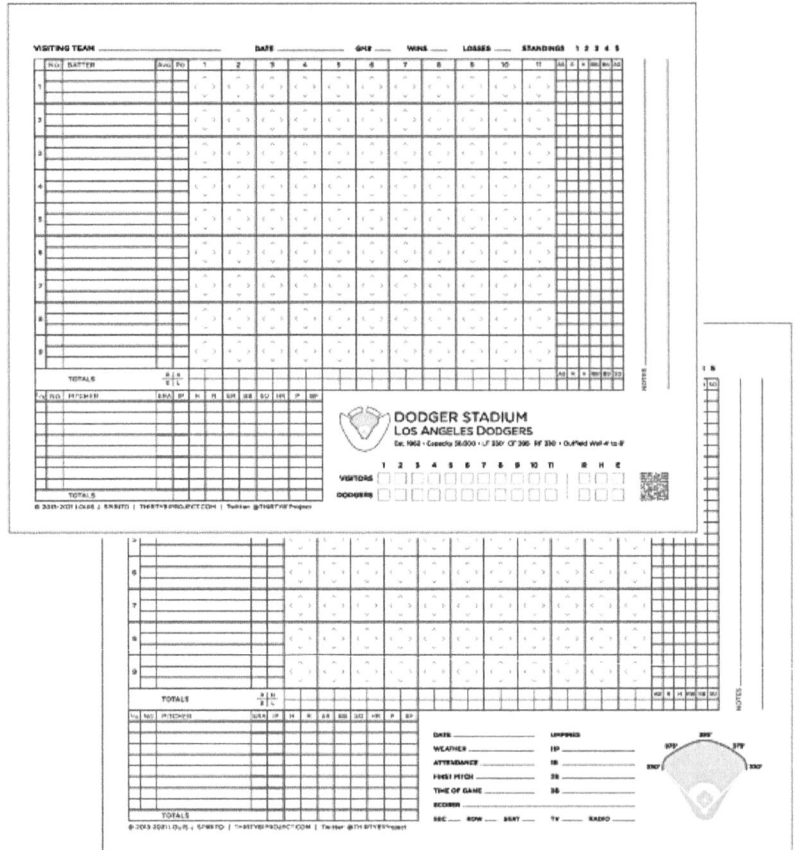

Scorecard design ©2013-2021 Louis J. Spirito | THIRTY81Project